Shaping Your Future

Shaping Your Future

Become the Brand Everyone Wants

Rita Rocker

BEP

BUSINESS EXPERT PRESS

Leader in applied, concise business books

Shaping Your Future: Become the Brand Everyone Wants

First published in 2021 by
Business Expert Press, LLC
222 East 46th Street, New York, NY 10017
www.businessexpertpress.com

ISBN-13: 978-1-95334-958-3 (paperback)
ISBN-13: 978-1-95334-959-0 (e-book)

Business Expert Press Business Career Development Collection

Collection ISSN: 2642-2123 (print)
Collection ISSN: 2642-2131 (electronic)

First edition: 2021

10 9 8 7 6 5 4 3 2 1

Description

This book is a powerful combination of transforming tools related to our three-part being: spirit, soul (will, intellect and emotions), and our body (what people observe, hear and the perceptions they form). What happens on the inside impacts every part of life on the outside. These exercises, stories, examples, and educational components are filled with techniques and inspiration designed to guide you into how to successfully advance your personal and professional life simultaneously. You will be empowered to learn how to turn both personal and professional challenges into success. These techniques can be implemented immediately and experienced for a lifetime.

Beginning with the very first chapter, you will launch into transforming exercises that dig deep to accelerate maximum growth. Become proficient as a routinely sought-after friend and business associate using this self-esteem, professional image, and business etiquette guidebook. Attract the most positive relationships by developing a success-driven default mindset through autosuggestion techniques. Confidently communicate with all socio-economic, educational and age groups. Learn powerful and effective communication skills to engage one or 1,000.

When you finish this book, you will revel in your new life and career reinvention, strength, reputation, persona and mind set. You will be empowered to radiate indispensable characteristics to those you meet every day. Start now!

Shaping Your Future Study Guide is highly recommended.

Keywords

career; powerful personal and professional image; verbal and non-verbal communication and presentation skills; mental GPS and autosuggestion techniques; life and career reinvention; notable credibility; branding yourself for success

Contents

Introduction

Welcome to *Shaping Your Future: Become the Brand Everyone Wants!*

*How we see ourselves and believe others see us will
determine where we end up in life!*

The most important attribute about this book is that it equally impacts both your personal life and career together in one package. Being fulfilled, successful, and considered indispensable in this world is a three-part mix of spirit, soul (our will, intellect, and emotions) and physical body (appearance, health, energy level, demeanor you project). What you have seen, felt, and heard from early on until today has an incredible effect on where you are now, your future choices, and where you will be next month and next year.

This may be a rather strange photo for a business guide, but the meaning is profound. That tiny dog saw itself as strong and spunky enough to chase the rhino, its goal being to go up against the *big guy*. It is a very good example to continue seeing ourselves as strong and capable enough to go after our dream, no matter what our current situation looks like.

IT'S ALL ABOUT ATTITUDE.

You can start changing what is going on around you when you begin changing what is *within* you!

Figure I.1 Rhino photo

Attitude and perception are everything when it comes to the choices we make, the individuals we associate with, and places where we spend our time. Your part in this world is very important. Your true calling is the one that genuinely resonates within you and gives you a sense of accomplishment and purpose. For some, that is financial gain, which is even more rewarding when used to help their fellow human beings. For others, it is a role that helps protect, educate, assist, build, entertain ... the list is endless.

Because all of life's experiences can either build us up or press and hold us down, this book begins with all about where you are on the *inside* and how mindsets can steer you in profoundly different directions by the thoughts and choices that we make. From there, we will explore what affects our *outer world*, whether our careers (fulfilled or not), our personal and professional relationships, business and personal finances, self-image makers and breakers, distinctive communication skills, and the persona we exude to everyone we come into contact with every day.

Stop often and reflect on how positive life choices will establish your inner and outer pathways to becoming the indispensable man or woman you truly are. Remind yourself each morning and throughout the day, especially when life gets tough, that you are crucial, vital, essential, necessary, and above all ... a VIP (valuable and important person)!!!

Use these stories and techniques as tools to begin employing immediately. They will last a lifetime! Rise!

Never compare your journey, credentials, accomplishments, (or any part of your life for that matter) with anyone else's.

When you measure your progress, only compare yourself to who you were yesterday.

Then get back on that ladder and take the next step divinely created for you.

Learn from others but never compare what you feel are your *liabilities* against their *assets*. Always focus on the massive amount of talents and gift you possess!

CHAPTER 1

Self-Assessment: Where You Are and Where Your Future Intentions Lie

You are the developer and designer of your life.

Where Your Life Is Now

The thoughts you entertain, words you speak, and the issues you write about are the major factors in where your life and career are today. Everything you think and do from this day forward will greatly affect where you will arrive in one year, five years, and for the rest of your life. Our belief system either helps us remove hindrances and prepare for success ahead or it keeps us down and defeated. The views and opinions we hold of ourselves (self-perception) and of the world around us create the way we *experience* reality. We devise in our minds, then follow through with our actions, whether we become successful in our own right or live with continuous disappointments.

We actively choose whether we have uplifting or degrading relationships, a career we enjoy, or mainly just have a *job* to survive. Even in the most devastating of times, we can seek and call forth peace, new associations, new opportunities, and the necessary support to make it to the other side. These thoughts and habits are critical to overcome on an almost daily basis. The characteristics we exhibit will, in turn, influence others to hire us for a new and better position, build community, and foster healthy relationships. When we replace the negative words we think, write, and speak, science has proven that we literally change how our brain functions and the kind of outcome our thoughts, words, and actions manifest.

A major shift in life's circumstances takes concentrating more on who you want to *become* and who you want to be *with* on a regular basis rather than what you actually do for a living or who currently surrounds you.

- What thoughts take up most of your time? Happy? Determined? Afraid of someone or something? Wishing for someone else's life or career, and how you can or cannot achieve it? Write them in a notebook.
- What do you believe *will* happen versus what *can* happen with clearer focus and more determination? Defeat? Gaining or losing something or someone very important to you? Taking classes or being mentored so that you can go after the kind of work you love?
- How long do you allow yourself to *feel* down or defeated? We all have bad days and hurtful thorns in life that stick us hard. These include all of the words we hear and read, disrespect from others, or perhaps a car that breaks down and no money to fix it.

Remember, how long you allow certain people, places, and things to affect your emotions is up to you. Have you ever taken a tough situation and said, "We're done here. No more. I now disconnect from this person, place, or thing. I am enrolling in a new class (for fun or career development), joining an organization where my talents can be used, or heading online to check out new cities?" Dream, take what action is needed in your life, one step at a time. Start *feeling* the exhilaration of moving forward. You can literally get that feeling by sitting quietly, closing your eyes, and visualizing how your *mental video* looks (place, people, activities, and so on), sounds, and makes you *feel*.

How Do You Speak to Yourself, See Yourself and Allow Yourself to Be Treated?

Write down what makes you feel:

- Confident and powerful: attention, appearance, health and vitality, relationships, finances, home, positive conversations

- Weak and ineffective: being dismissed by others, lack of finances or the education you believe you need for your area of interest, poor health or appearance, uncomfortable talking with others, and so on

Now you have the start of a *bucket list* of areas to begin changing. What you focus on you empower—*you become*! Center your thoughts on arriving at your thriving new destination, not on where you may be currently. As you concentrate on the new, you will be amazed how the old habits fade farther back until one day—they are no longer a detrimental part of your life!

No one can make you feel inferior without your permission.

—Eleanor Roosevelt

When thinking about where you currently are in life, if you feel reaching your goals is not really an option, check out these true life examples to stimulate your move forward. You can design your future just like these amazing individuals did:

Famous *Failures*

- *The Beatles* were rejected by Decca Records who said, "We don't like their sound" and "They have no future in show business."
- *Albert Einstein* was not able to speak until he was almost four years old and his teachers said he would "never amount to much."
- *Oprah Winfrey* was demoted from her job as a news anchor because she "wasn't fit for television."
- *Michael Jordan*, after being cut from his high-school basket-ball team, went home, locked himself in his room and cried.
- *Walt Disney* was fired from a newspaper for "lacking imagina-tion" and "having no original ideas." He and his brother grew up very poor on a dairy farm, laboring from very early in the morning until late at night, leaving no time to study, play,

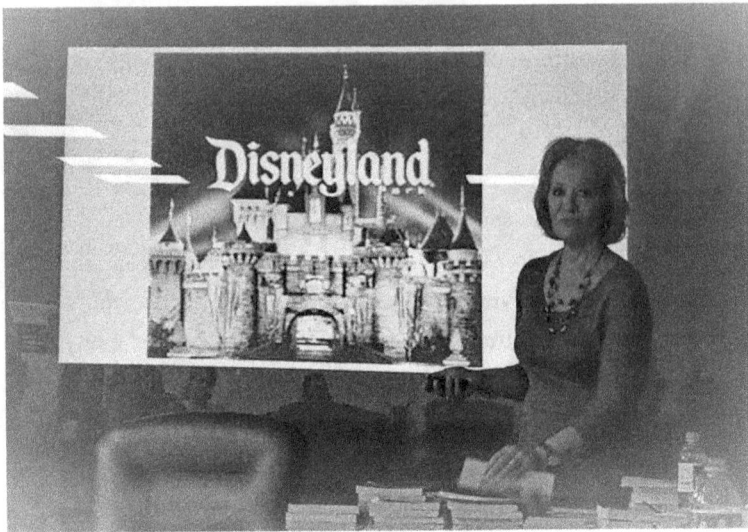

Figure 1.1 Disney Photo and Speaker

Source: SOARINGHIGHER.ROCKS

or rest. His father abused them if they did not get enough done. Walt wanted to create a place for people to have fun. He did!

- *Steve Jobs*, at age 30, was left devastated and defeated after being abruptly removed from the company *he* started. He rose again and became one of the most successful men in the world.
- *Grandma Moses* began painting at the age of 76 because her arthritis prevented her from using a needle for her embroidery! *Life* magazine put her on its cover to celebrate her 100th birthday. Her first painting that sold for three U.S. dollars later sold for 10,000 U.S. dollars.
- *Colonel Sanders* was in his 60s and on Social Security when he had to close his service station, but then set out to promote his secret chicken recipe after numerous devastating personal and business setbacks.
- *Barbara Hillary* became the first black woman to reach the North Pole at the age of 75.
- *Harry Bernstein* published his first book, *The Invisible Wall*, at age 96 in 2007.

- *Mary Hardison* became the oldest woman to do a tandem paraglide at 101. Now, that is determination at its best!
- *A former Miss Teen USA* was living with a foster mother and had no money for beautiful clothes or impressive finery and yet won the title with a 39 U.S. dollars gown and the belief that she was a strong, talented, and worthy young lady. She is an excellent role model for not letting her circumstances keep her from her dream.
- *A teenager living in poverty* received a scholarship to Harvard after living through her junior high and high-school days in shelters with her mother.

How is this for unfettered determination? A California man who missed his 1942 graduation because he was locked in an internment camp for Japanese-Americans during the Second World War finally fulfilled his dream. The L.A. Times reported that 89-year-old Don Miyada walked with the Class of 2014 at Newport Harbor High School 72 years after he was denied his own cap and gown. Talk about life's circumstances getting in the way!!! He never let go until his dream came to pass!

Old ways of doing things will not open new, different doors! Remember the saying: If you always do what you've always done, you'll always get what you've always had.

Hit the "reset" button and kick your way out of the box you no longer want to be part of!

Just as the preceding examples prove, when you allow yourself to go through a life-transforming metamorphosis (a striking change in appearance, character, or circumstances), it is because you either realize you have grown too much to stay where you are or you cannot allow yourself to suffocate in the familiar, constricting cocoon any longer! *Others can help you or hurt you, but they cannot "be" your self-respect or confident self-image.* On those days when you may be disappointed with yourself, look beyond your mirror and remember that you are made in a most divine image— the most powerful and magnificent image there is! Build yourself up by speaking respectfully to, and about, yourself even when you do not feel like it. The results of your new intentions will astound you.

It is in your moments of decision that your destiny is shaped.
—Anthony Robbins

Back to the Future

Close your eyes and create! When we look around with our eyes wide open, we see the world and our life's situation, finances, relationships, and so on as they currently exist. If any of those areas are in disheartening shape, it is difficult to imagine and recreate a life of fulfilled dreams and purpose. Thinking quietly with our eyes closed ignites our imagination of what can be, instead of what is at present. Try it with *relaxing* instrumental music. Focus on the opportunities and possibilities instead of present obstacles in order to unlock your inner architect.

Start at the End of Your Life and Create Your Plan in Reverse!

As you work toward your personal reinvention, start with where you truly want to be if your wildest dreams were achieved. Okay, remember Walt Disney. This will help you explore fresh possibilities, new relationships, programs, and steps to take to reach that goal. Work backward, beginning with your end goal at the top. Add a picture at the top of the ladder of what you want to be doing. Include pictures of how you want to interact with others. Want to be a successful speaker? Show one where the audience is completely engaged with your message. New home? Put it there. New career? Add a photo of a happy, determined person doing what you love. From there, list stair steps that include your business classes, personal and professional relationship changes and additions, organizations to become active in. As you take steps upward from the bottom rung, add anything new or different that comes to mind.

It is always helpful to read the biographies of well-known scientists, politicians, entertainers, and so on to acquire a better understanding of how they continued to raise the bar with each new action step. There is nothing more invigorating, faith-building, or obstacle-crushing than to mentally see your final goal manifested, no matter what life looks like now. *"Seeing" the end is how we "get" to the end!*

Often, our greatest rejection causes our greatest direction.

—Joel Osteen

Journal every day. Create positive thoughts where frustrating circumstances emerge.

"I get to plan my day because I am in charge of what happens to me. I will deal appropriately with anyone or anything that seeks to upset my day. This is my day and I can overcome!"

First step: Create your ultimate goal page. Take the time to write out in great detail:

- How you want to look and feel: confident, strong, engaging, respected, as an excellent communicator, appealing, as an authority figure, and so on.
- What you want your bank account to be and how you intend to use it.
- What kind of family and social life *you* truly want. If individuals in homeless shelters or without limbs can conquer obstacles and create a rewarding life, so can you.

Positive Characteristics

- List the attributes you have now like creativity, strength, your business skills (negotiator, craftsman, science whiz, creative designer, gourmet cook, caring mentor), and so forth.
- Record the traits necessary to exchange in order to reach those goals. These may include replacing negative friends or individuals on the job (when possible) with supportive ones. Possibly exchange something like watching four hours of television after work for participating in educational programs that will help get you to the next level.
- Add a desired completion date at the top of the page with small steps you can take each week to rebuild, restore, redistribute, or revise your current habits and lifestyle. Enter a date for the completion of each step. Close your eyes before you go to sleep at night and see it happening. Visualize your positive

changes each morning before you get out of bed. The more you *see* it, the sooner it can show up.

If you feel like a fish out of water, stop! Change directions. Find a new river to swim in. BE who "you" were designed to be. Do not deny yourself, develop yourself.

Where You Want Your Life to Be

- *What do I wish to change?* Health? Finances? Career? Neighborhood? These can include frustrations, embarrassing issues, your car or home, type of job you tolerate rather than enjoy, and so on.
- What friends, family members, jobs, or other areas in my life need to be replaced? How can I change what I am doing and who I am spending time with? Be detailed with constructive and feasible steps. This includes the word *No.* Another example is to bring your own coffee container and snacks to work and save all of that money for a couple of new outfits.
- Examine your relationships. Detrimental associations damage self-esteem. Constant negative feedback wears you down. Change can be frightening, yet very rewarding. Cultivate positive new alliances. That step alone can change your life, giving you the reputation of an indispensable friend and teammate! Praying for new friends really does work!
- What will it take to transform your life? Letting go of anyone or anything that holds you back? An exercise and eating plan for increased energy and self-esteem? Classes (technical, marketing, image, finance, and so on) that will equip you for your new position?
- Who can help you get to the next step? Who or where can you turn to for support? Teacher? Pastor? Friend? Community leader? Mentor? Make a list of possibilities and then *ask.* Do it this week. These can include frustrations, embarrassing

issues, your car or home. The prerequisite to asking is possibly to swallow our pride or to overcome fear of rejection. I speak from experience. As the Godfather Pizza spokesperson says, "Just do it!"

- What is preventing you from stepping into your new life? Are they perceived or real roadblocks? Be honest. Many people unknowingly allow the fear of failure, rejection, or abandonment to hold them back. Even if you are in a difficult place at present, see who can barter time or a service with you. This can be trading one of your skills (cooking, bookkeeping, coaching, and so on) in exchange for a trusted person to take care of your loved one a few hours per week. Make it a win–win situation.

- As far as old, damaging thoughts are concerned, write them down. Examples include "My teacher said I would never succeed" or "My former boss said no one would ever want me again at another company." One of the most important points in this book is that *no* one's words have the right to determine your worth and abilities. No one! Repeat … *no* one!

- If you cannot completely change a particular area of your life (currently a caregiver, being in a rough financial situation, having a physical hindrance), what steps can you take to make it better? Begin with one realistic step, then the next, and the next. This may include a temporary second job to save up enough money for a place of your own. It could be exchanging 30 minutes a day of television for exercise to get those endorphins revved up. Endorphins can trigger positive feelings and help relieve stress. Stop and look up to the sky … smile. Does that not immediately change your emotional state for the better? Go!

Nowadays, virtual meetings and education are a normal part of life, which aids those who are not able to get to the events otherwise in order to build new relationships. As the old saying goes, "Rome was not built in a day." Neither were we. It is a steady process and well worth the transforming work. Okay, look up and smile again!!

If you are not being treated with love and respect, check your price tag.
Perhaps you have marked yourself down. It is YOU who tells people
what you are worth by what you accept. Get off the clearance rack
and get behind the glass where the valuables are kept. Learn to value
yourself. If you don't, no one else will!

—Author Unknown.

You just moved yourself to the case where the valuables are kept, right?

Steps to *Remove* Obstacles on the Road to Your New Destination

Many individuals keep up partitions in their lives and look for reasons something cannot be done, whether competing for a new career or moving to a new company or city where the opportunities they truly desire are waiting. What is the transformation you are seeking? A negative situation can be painful and so unfulfilling but ... it is familiar! We stick to it even if we are trying to get out of that box. We may possibly think that there is no risk of failure or rejection *if* we stay in what is familiar, but is there? Everyday. Self-esteem plays a major role in arriving where we want to be. This means having *self*-respect and knowing our *self*-worth. Remember to never go back to the clearance rack if it has been a familiar place.

We all want to achieve our special dreams; however, over the years, our lives often take a different course, filled to overflowing with work and relationships that leave little or no time to pursue our original goals. We often begin thinking about all of the reasons why we cannot attain those dreams due to any number of circumstances. Some of those reasons may be legitimate for a reason; others are based on fear or lack of self-confidence. The more time and energy we expend entertaining those reasons, the farther we get from grabbing our own brass ring, the symbol of a goal that was conquered by reaching up and grabbing it.

What must be removed or adjusted to clear your path? Think about your personal responsibilities and limits that you must set while heading toward the goal line. They may incorporate the following:

- Set healthy new boundaries of what you will and will not accept. These can include how you will allow others to treat you, how you need to build your career, and that you will not accept mediocrity in any form.
- Determine if a flattering new look or more professional image would make you feel better and conduct yourself with more confidence. If hiring a consultant is not in your current budget, go online and check out professional images, wardrobes, verbal and non-verbal communications that make an impressive persona … the list is endless.
- Take classes for personal and career growth in whatever way builds your self-esteem and technical skills.

The one who has the most power to change your life is the one you see in your mirror!

Holding on to negative past events is a process that can destroy your life and career advancement in ways you may not even be aware of. Ask yourself these questions. Do the feelings and habits I am retaining:

- Serve any worthwhile purpose
  - For me?
  - For my family?
  - For my career?
- Help me
  - Move forward with my goals?
  - Hold me back in my uncomfortable comfort zone?
  - Why or why not?
- Work in my favor in any way?
  - Why or why not?

How you answered these questions will tell you a lot about what you need to do to get in the fast lane of transformation. If those emotions and thoughts do not help you, focus and move.

Write out in great detail where you are now and where you choose to be:

Table where you are now

	Where you are now	What must change
How you want to look and feel		
What kind of family life you want		
What kind of social life you want		
What you will feel like and how life will be after this situation, person, or thing is no longer negatively impacting your life		

Affirmation: I am *slamming the door on the past:* Self-sabotage *does not live here anymore! Regret, defeat and all other hindrances have now left the building!*

That door is locked and can NEVER enter my life again!!

CHAPTER 2

Create Your Success-Driven Mental GPS Through Autosuggestion Techniques

Many of us have experienced a rough life and followed self-sabotaging behaviors because it was all we knew growing up. All of that stressful commotion was not pleasant but was familiar and seemingly *normal*. These experiences can include destructive words we receive and accept, abusive treatment from those closest to us, staying in an unhealthy home or job, or associating with negative and toxic friendships. Patterns develop that can continue through life if not uncovered, faced head on, dealt with, and transformed. In some ways, turmoil can be comforting only because it is familiar, *not* because it is good for us.

No matter how crazy life can be, we have the ability to make choices that will alter our circumstances. Practicing autosuggestion techniques of stating the exact opposite of what you are thinking can quickly change habits and behaviors. Examples include turning the words and thoughts of being a failure to being incredibly successful. Yes, say it and think it. Help those around you do the same thing. Remember those famous failures in Chapter 1? Change "Oh, I'm never going to lose weight" to "I am in excellent shape and truly desire to eat healthy and get lots of energizing exercise." "I am never going to be able to compete with other golfers, educators, business owners" to "I love this area of my life and am rapidly growing to be one of the best in this field. My focus is strong and I am determined to finish strong!"

Figure 2.1 Breakthrough glass

Pushing Through to Your New Destiny

Have you ever felt your environment immediately change when some-one walked into a room? This energy can be very positive and pique your interest or feel like an icy fog rolled in. People often do not realize they are exuding or releasing a specific energy to others. Avoid bringing negative energy from past adverse events and emotions into the pres-ent, as they only attract more of the same. Focusing on more construc-tive behaviors attracts positive situations and respectful treatment. *The excitement of realizing you no longer accept what you would have in the past is exhilarating to say the least!* Life's experiences hold powerful les-sons but should never be the determining factor of where you are going from here.

Whether from reality TV, our cell phones, or social networking, we have become a society that skips from one stimulating experience (whether good or bad) to the next, rarely wondering why we crave so much excitement on a continuous basis. Rarely do we give ourselves a break long enough to consider why we need constant distractions, and therefore, continue avoiding taking the steps necessary to remove chaotic or self-defeating lifestyles and events.

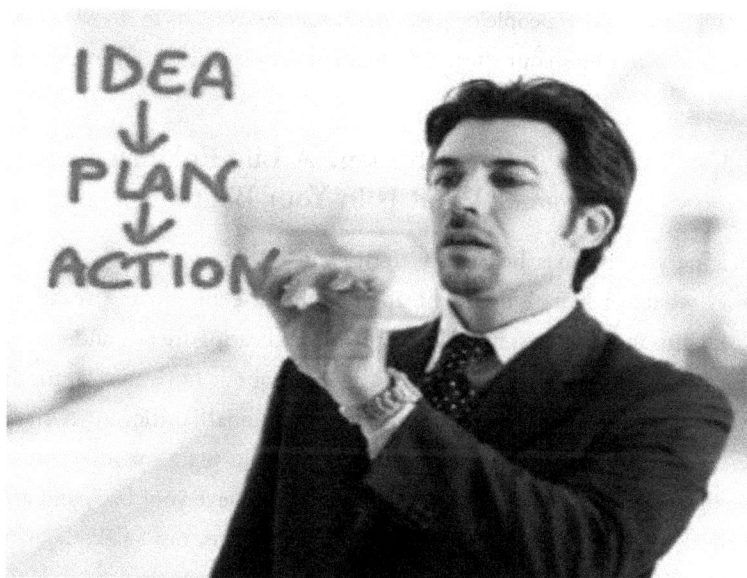

Figure 2.2 Idea–plan–action

Others may seek to influence your life in ways that cause turmoil, chaos, or uncomfortable encounters that you really should not have to live with. It is then that you determine:

- Yes, but this is okay and for the good of my family, myself, and my future. It will have a positive effect. Why?
- No, this is not okay and will cause more disruption, financial loss, pain, and so on.
- I need more information to convince me this is a favorable experience or relationship. This is what I need to do next. This may include initiating a serious talk with someone, checking out new jobs on the Web, and so on.

Needing to move on in a different direction is something you most likely will face several times in your life. You may want to hold on to people or situations that have walked away from you or negatively affected you; however, you can also make the deliberate choice to create new life patterns, ones that reflect a dignified, healthy self-image and beneficial relationships in this global economy. Moving forward does not really have as much to do with people or past circumstances as it has to do with *how you* choose to build your spirited life, one dynamic brick at a time.

Do You Have a Growth Plan? A Life Enhancement Game? What Is in Your Boat?

Imagine you are in a boat away from shore. What would you pack to cover whatever situations might appear? Safety equipment? Instead of flashlights and blankets, it could be reliable and caring friends and family or a saving account or a healthier body. What about fun and relaxation? What does your life's adventure consist of? A Global Positioning System (GPS) to explore *new* places? Life jacket (plans in place for unexpected events)? Beer and bad relationships? Friends who have your back and are there to support you or ones who would knock you out of the boat if they did not get their way? Stressful people and burdens that weigh your boat down? Companions and associates who have a good sense of humor? Those who are always grouchy and negative? What we plan for the future is like packing a boat. What happens if an emergency strikes? What happens if the boat breaks down or we run out of gas? Lay out your plan for life. Do you keep it? Toss it? Fix it?

> Where you end up in life is more about Choices than Circumstances!

The circumstances, outcomes, and relationships in your life are many times a reflection of the choices you (or others) have made *with* you or *for* you along the way. These experiences can create either a healthy, victorious value system or one that exacerbates chaos, disappointment, and failure.

Although there are no actual *physical* restraints over our minds, there are so many words, recollections, and events that can still bind us to old impairing habits and beliefs. Dwelling on our shortcomings and fears just makes those imaginary hindrances stronger and more difficult to replace. It takes willingness to consistently change our self-talk every time we think or say something not in our best interest. Disarray is tenacious, but so are we! It can be overcome! Consider how you will handle future situations and people who could take away your power or make you feel uncomfortable. What are other options, choices, or responses? Sometimes, strong body language and direct eye contact can make a strong statement without saying a word.

I once read an interesting study about the barracuda and mackerel, the barracuda's favor dining delight. Researchers put them in a large tank with a glass partition in between. For three days, the ferocious predator constantly banged its nose into the glass trying to claim his delectable prize. At the end of the third day, he gave up. At this point, the researchers removed the partition between them so that the mackerel could easily become dinner. What do you think happened? Nothing! In its little fish brain, the barracuda could not have what it had fought so hard for and gave up even though the prize was there for the taking.

How many times in our lives do we give in too soon even though we were one step away from our destination? Sometimes people look for partitions in their own lives and believe they were not good enough or smart enough. Elephants, the largest land mammals, are often bound to chains as babies so that they never realize when they are large and powerful, they could actually overcome what confines them. Give this some thought in your own life if a human story like this exists. You are strong, you are intelligent, and you are worthy of greatness!!

Jump into the sea of limitless creative opportunities. *Author* your plans for recreating thriving new areas of your life—spirit, soul, and body. Look how free our adventurous friends are in this picture. What did it take to transform their situation? They had to:

1. Admit they were not willing to stay in their confined, limited little world any longer
2. Focus on what they wanted and needed to recreate their lives and took the big leap of faith
3. They carefully devised their plan and then jumped higher than ever before, over the wall to an amazing new start even if they did it afraid.

Did those fish have the choice of staying in those limited boundaries that the small but familiar bowl (people, jobs, lower education, and so on) provided? Yes, but they decided to make the ascent to the new high road. Wow, free at last to explore their new destiny.

Think about the limiting place you may be in right now and then look at where you really want to be: graduating from college no matter what a parent or teacher told you; excelling in international business; enjoying a healthy and happy relationship; having that career your personality, temperament, and cultural norms were made for. If you want desperately to skyrocket out of limitations, think of the fish. Envision the *other side* of where you are now. Your mental GPS may be saying "Excuse me! You need to take a right turn at this corner" (your new decision).

Plunge (taken from my keynote *How to Swim When Your Ship is Sinking*) into the wellspring of new life, liberating yourself from negative relationships, thoughts, actions, and the words and behaviors of others. Let go off the struggle, of the current view you or others have of your life, and head onward and upward. Heroes do it even when afraid. So can you!

When you visualize, particularly in the times that are the most disappointing or frightening, that new road you seek. Literally picture what you plan to see on that road (*obstacles* and *opportunities*) with the right ending in mind. See new people (partner, special friend, and so on), a new home (the one you really want, not what you feel you can afford on your current salary), a nicer car, a rewarding social life filled with good and supportive people, communicating with individuals from around the world right from your desk. Wow! Use your senses of sight, sound, touch, and hearing to make it even more real.

What are the warning signs of hindering weights (smoldering embers, so to speak) that could be keeping you from soaring up to where you belong?

- "I do not look good enough, am not thin enough, or have nice enough clothes." Well, I have been a bargain shopper all of my life. You can do it too!
- "I do not have enough education to do what I truly want." Just about anything you want or need to learn is free on YouTube or in blogs.

Figure 2.3 Cat and tiger

- "I am not worthy of any good thing. Everyone said so." Like I said before, never *allow* anyone's opinion tell you what you are capable of accomplishing or what your worth is.

You are more than a conqueror and of great value!

Those thoughts should no longer have permission to linger. Yes, we do give them permission. No, they do not! Not anymore!

"The one who has the most power to change your life is the one in your mirror!"

It is an undeniable fact: the kind of seeds you sow, you *will* also reap. Planting a peach tree will never give us corn. Keep nourishing your *growth* seeds (your spirit, soul, and body), and you will see a transition take place.

It is a law of nature that you manifest what you plant. It is a law of creation as well! Your choice of seeds may include the following.

How Long You Allow Others to Affect Your Emotions Is up to You

- How do you speak to yourself: kindly, angrily, respectfully, critically, with praise for the effort, and so on?
- How do you see yourself: bold, strong, happy, sad, confident, too fat or thin, classy, frumpy, tired, motivated, fun, and so on?
- How do you allow yourself to be regarded? With respect, contempt from others, torn down, built up, positive treatment only?
- What makes you feel confident and powerful? Constructive and positive conversations, ability to gain new business, appearance, fitness level, well educated, maintaining an attitude of success, and the drive to arrive at your destination? If you are at a red light, hang in there. Green is coming!
- What makes you feel weak and ineffective? How you grew up, words and actions of others, appearance, finances, lack of self-esteem, and feelings of worthiness.
- How you will handle future situations that could take away your power or make you feel uncomfortable? As Glinda in the Wizard of Oz said, "My dear, you have had the power within you all along." Believe it!

Overcoming fear, disorder and disappointments to compete in our amazing world

Disorder: Unrest, confusion, commotion, disarray, turmoil, unruly

Disappointment: regret, setbacks, disillusionment

Circumstances: Situations, settings, surroundings, positions

Choices: Deliberate decisions to *create* stability, calm, harmony, peace, orderliness, organization

Disappointment and failures, in this case, refer to a lifestyle of disorder or confusion. A person who lives in that continuous state (even unintentionally) accepts an odd sort of comfort in disarray, disharmony, or disorder. Upheaval and confusion may even provide a warped sense of security because that is what we have known, and thus, it is familiar. Another reason for the false sense of security is because, subconsciously, we believe it is what we deserve. Nothing could be further from the truth. Those types of feelings tell us we are *replaceable*. The real truth is that you are definitely indispensable! Always be aware you can change your mental GPS!

Often, we subconsciously attract hectic schedules, destructive lifestyles, binge eating, too much alcohol, or other self-defeating behaviors because it helps us hide from what is really going on in our lives (lack of self-esteem, fear of failure, lost jobs, and so on). Unfortunately, when we choose not to deal with the pain or fear we feel, it can eventually ruin our lives. Continuously remind yourself that you are crucial to the world, your career, and to those around you.

Questions to Ask for Acquiring and Maintaining an Indispensable Reputation Through Redirecting Your Mental GPS

- What was my reason for that particular decision or behavior? Was any of it based out of fear? Lack of interest on my side or theirs? Because it was the easy way out, although not the best, most efficient, or thoughtful way to handle it?
- Did their response have any merit at all? Cheaper? Quicker? Easier? Unethical? Was it strictly self-seeking?
- How does their rejection or disapproval affect my job? Image? Feelings of worth? Status with others? Take time to examine this in depth.
- How can I show a strong yet positive outlook in spite of it? What is the most effective way to communicate to bring this situation back to a workable solution? Should I send a letter or make a call with positive problem resolutions in hand? Yes, always offer resolution suggestions.

- There are times when seizing the reins is appropriate, but there are times when letting go can be beneficial. Releasing the reins creates a more empowered employee, teammate, or family member who provides you the opportunity to truly learn and grow from the experience. When an associate seizes the moment to take on a task or project that normally would have been completed by someone in a higher position, their engagement level increases and self-esteem is boosted.

Next time negativity happens, stop and immediately *shift* your thoughts. Literally, lift your head upward and begin. It feels like nurturing sunshine on your face.

> *When you allow what someone says or does to upset you, you're allowing that* person to control you.
>
> —Joel Osteen

Your answers to the following questions can be life- and career-changing. Does your GPS need to be adjusted? Ask yourself:

- "If I were viewing myself from another person's perspective, would I want to have me for a manager, client, business partner?" Why or why not?
- Would my appearance, manner, speech, and behavior exhibit the kind of characteristics that would prompt me to want a personal or business relationship with myself? Why or why not?

Build a powerful reputation at work and in your community. As the famous Mary Kay Ash used to say, "Look at each person as if they have a sign around their neck that says, 'Please make me feel important!'"

Compare Your Mental GPS to a Kaleidoscope

1. An instrument that contains loose fragments or bits and pieces that change and exhibit its contents in an endless variety of varicolored forms. How? By turning it to a new picture.

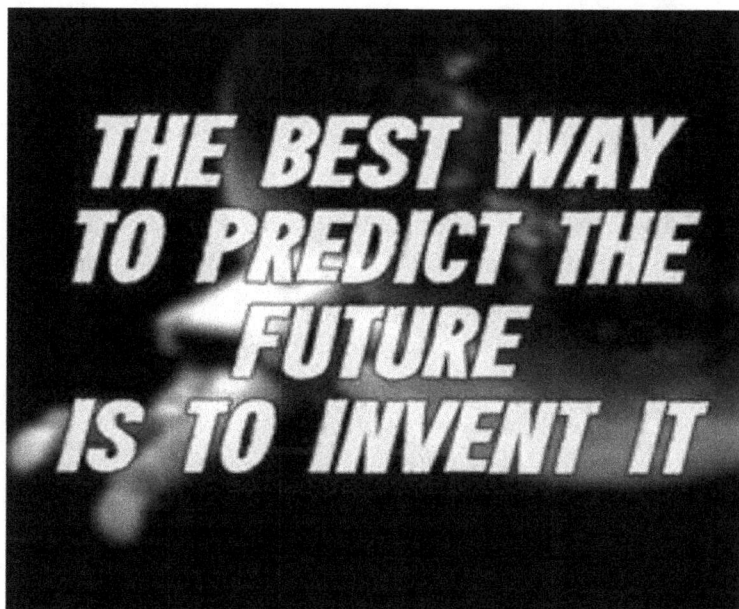

Figure 2.4 Predict future

2. A succession of changing phases or actions constantly changing, rapidly shifting.

Life can seem like a mass of disjointed bits and pieces having no particular significance by themselves, but you can recreate a fulfilling new picture by bringing them together to make a masterpiece. Keep adjusting until it does.

The best accomplishments usually occur when a person's body or mind is stretched to its limits in a voluntary effort to accomplish something difficult and worthwhile.

—Mihaly Csikzentdhalyi

Recreating Your Life: From Unpredictability to Consistency

Society in general, and all forms of media, are constantly voicing their opinion of what they think is acceptable, fashionable, enjoyable, popular, and politically correct. What are the greatest influencers, people, situations, and circumstances, that have led you down the paths that represent your current life? Think about each one. It begins with our home environment, parents, siblings, and other relatives. Next come peers and friends, including neighbors and school mates. Careless or judgmental words, opinions, and actions will never have the right to determine where you end up in life. In all reality, that choice is yours!

Depending on what influencers we have had in our lives, we see favorable or unfavorable habits, choices, and outcomes as *normal*, because that was just part of our everyday life. Maybe we grew up in a good home with lots of love, or we may have had the opposite experience and endured one that had destructive or unhealthy tendencies passed down through generations. One common trait is that of instability. Escaping the life cycles we inherited is important not only for our well-being but that of our families, careers, and relationships. When we break out of poverty or a painful relationship, by autosuggestion, we must speak to ourselves in a positive, transforming, and encouraging word (new job, uplifting friend, kind gesture, people initiating new relationships), it helps us see that life has many more good experiences than we have experienced so far. However, we can be so afraid of the unknown that we revert back to self-sabotaging behaviors that bring us back to that *familiar place* that we have strived to climb out of for so long. Let the powerful voice within you rise up and say, *Not THIS time, we are done here! I am intelligent, capable, motivated, high quality, and rising to my greater destiny.*

Think of your mind as a computer with several applications open, including all of the items listed in the preceding figure. Work diligently to program it for the most positive and effective transformation. Just like a computer, if you load the wrong software into your mind, it will not function correctly and may cause a *hardware* crash (illness, bankruptcy, job loss) that can produce an aggravating or disappointing setback. This leads to taking more time and effort to restore what was damaged before you can rebuild self-esteem or finances again. Just like when a computer gets a virus and must be cleaned up, we often need to remove the negative *viruses* in our lives. They run the gamut from adverse and demoralizing work or personal relationships, bad health habits that tear us down, careless spending that can put us in a sea of debt, and just plain filling our mind's computer with self-defeating *trash*. When our thoughts become

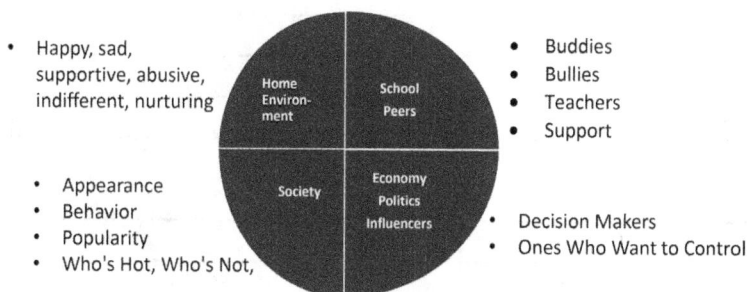

- Happy, sad, supportive, abusive, indifferent, nurturing

Home Environ-ment

School Peers

- Buddies
- Bullies
- Teachers
- Support

- Appearance
- Behavior
- Popularity
- Who's Hot, Who's Not,

Society

Economy Politics Influencers

- Decision Makers
- Ones Who Want to Control

Figure 2.5 Corner graph

infected, we either clean them up and go forward in victory mode or clog up our system and sit in limbo wishing for a calmer and more productive life. It is your choice to replace your mental software with new, updated programs as needed. This is a never-ending process. Mentally create your vision of being an essential and successful owner, employee, partner, client ... you name it!

Experts say it takes 21 days to form a new habit. Can you resolve to see yourself confident, healthier, in a flourishing new relationship, financially stronger, or whatever your need or desire is, for the next 21 days? Can you make that specific period of time one of *seeing* and *feeling* what you truly want to happen *as if* it has manifested already? Allow your pliable, magnificent brain to create a mental *blueprint* of what you want to accomplish. Even if you cannot see *how* to get to the end result, do not worry about that right now. Only concentrate on *seeing* and *believing*. Your brain can then begin to shift into the behaviors (positive, confident, more tolerant, analytical where needed, engaging, and so on) and means necessary to attract and complete this vision.

For the next 21-day habit transformation, begin each day with an attitude of *expecting* the best rather than just hoping something bad does not happen. Disappointments occur, and sometimes, we get bad news. However, it is important to steer your day in the most positive way possible, even if you have to redirect your thought pattern several times. Call out and declare the best to happen to you—redirect it and *expect* it. Determine the greatest day possible.

Day	Where was my focus?	What did I feel/accomplish?	Goal for tomorrow
1			
2			
3			
4			
5			
6			
7			
8			
9			
10			
11			
12			
13			
14			
15			
16			
17			
17			
19			
20			
21			

Figure 2.6 21-day plan

Reprogram Your Mind

It is easy to live down to critical, self-fulfilling prophecies placed on us by parents, teachers, or others. These words and behaviors can make us fearful to step out and change those things that will bring us to a new life of peace and prosperity. One thing I learned after years of detrimental patterns was *We do not have to go through life that way. No one's opinion, careless words, or actions, whether family, employer, or everyone else you know, have the right to determine our future!* They are just words, and often-times, the individual saying them had no idea how much damage those words could do! Mental tapes can be replaced, as often as necessary, to totally reshape your thoughts and choices! That is where intentionally seeking new friends, classes, and positive affirmations can help move you in a different, more beneficial direction. The massive amount of inspiring, motivational communications on the Internet has the ability to help reprogram your thoughts, even if those around you cannot, or will not, contribute to your continuous rise.

Your Brain and the Power of Belief

It is a scientific fact that the power of belief can cause the brain to lead the entire body in a certain way, good or bad. What mental tapes are you listening to? How many of them need to be pulled out, crushed to dust, and tossed in the trash? Stop to think about where you are now and what thoughts and experiences got you there. Do you still hear any of the following mental tapes playing in your head that continue to create damage? "You will never amount to anything." "Who do you think you are? You can't do that." "Nobody is ever going to want you" or "You have nothing to offer." Are you feeling like life let you down? Are you in a financial crisis? Do you have friends or a partner who want to keep you down on their level, way below where your talents and abilities really lie?

Ever look at a packet of flower seeds and see a beautiful and full array of gorgeous flowers? Yet, when you open the packet, what do the seeds look like initially? They are shriveled and ugly, right? You plant them in the ground, alone, away from any light or sunshine. They just get *rained on* in the beginning (like what happens in life quite often), but what is going on beneath the surface? Just like your own building blocks you are painstakingly setting in place (educational classes, replacing negative friends, a new exercise program), caring for the seeds of your dreams of being loved and respected in this world will eventually cause the *fruit of your labor* to surface just like those flowers.

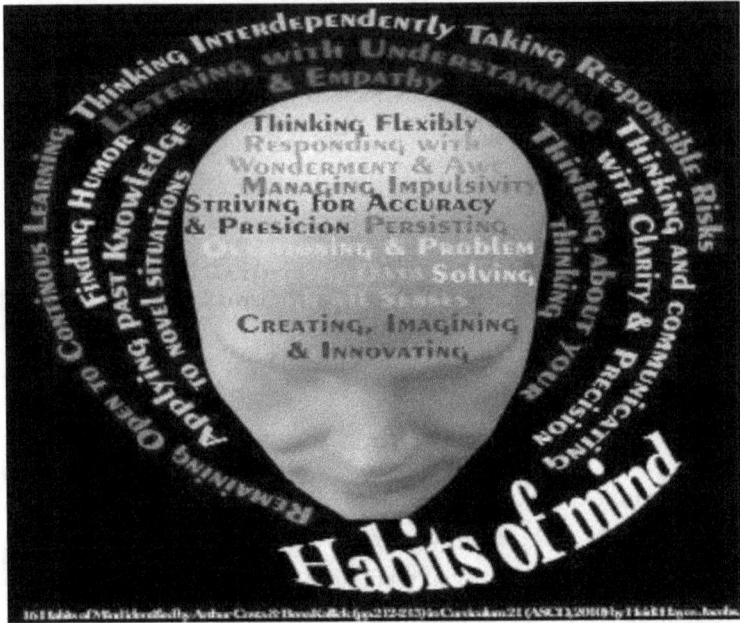

Figure 2.7 Brain—habits of mind

Each morning when I open my eyes, I say to myself: I, not events, have the power to make me happy or unhappy today. I can choose which it shall be. Yesterday is dead and tomorrow has not arrived yet. I have just one day, today, and I am going to be happy in it.

—Groucho Marx

Positive mental attitude and our personalities consist of the following:

Keeping a flexible, positive mental attitude can be achieved so that the comments or actions of others cannot take control of your day or most certainly your life. You cannot control what others say or do; however, you can control how you react. Determine to always be in tune to how successful people do not get drawn into other people's attitudes or actions. One way is if you know a conversation is coming up that will negatively affect you, prepare mentally ahead of time by rehearsing, or setting the scene. Think about the issue at hand, what stance you believe they will take, and what they may say. If you are having a discussion in person, watch their body language for clues: sadness, fear, anger, hostility, and so on. List any key points they will possibly bring up, positive and negative. See yourself with controlled posture, confidence in your body signals and voice. What are the most effective words, scenarios, and the ultimate, workable problem resolution you can provide to help quell the situation without pulling you into a confrontation or damaging both your self-image and theirs?

Traits that Destroy a Pleasing Personality

- *Interrupting.* Winning etiquette says to speak 40 percent and listen 60 percent. When we interrupt, we are giving the message that ours is the only opinion that matters. It also shows that we are not listening but only wanting to interject our thoughts.
- *Unnecessary pessimism*, skepticism, or distrust. A combination of (1) facts plus (2) sensitivity goes a tremendously long way for the most positive relationships.
- *Self-important, prideful, or egocentric behavior* in words or actions can destroy relationships. Building others up actually builds you up in their eyes. Even if we do not agree, we must show genuine care and concern for other people's thoughts and feelings.
- *False flattery.* The attempt to flatter, especially when it is not deserved, may be interpreted by some as manipulation. People love *sincere* compliments. A person of strength also appreciates a constructive critique when it helps them to learn and grow to the next level. Most individuals know *in their gut* if they are receiving manipulative comments or sincere, deserved kudos.
- *Negative attitudes* that find fault with the world in general and interject negative comments into most conversations discover their circle of friends and business associates will often grow smaller over time. It is important to deal with disapproving issues with strong, positive actions. Offer your constructive suggestions for resolution.
- *Confrontational or argumentative* behaviors for the sake of always having the upper hand can be damaging to one's

reputation. Alpha males and females are people tending to assume a dominant or domineering role in social or professional situations. This role may be established from a young age for protection or to feel valued as being stronger than others. That type of force or pressure can also repel others as it does not allow them to express their own beliefs and opinions. Even if someone's thoughts cannot be applied, it is important to acknowledge them. If something will not work, explain why.

- *Giving unwelcome advice* that is intrusive and appears controlling will often, although not always, create negative feelings. When I was younger and working for my state government, my mentor from a modeling school told me I sounded very harsh and unprofessional when answering the telephone. At first, I was somewhat offended but swallowed my pride and started listening to the impression my phone manners were giving. She was right! It was a very important lesson that changed my telephone manners from that day forward. Sage advice: accept what is *constructive* criticism and toss out everything else. Always think: Does this benefit me in any way? If so, I will accept it and make the necessary changes to improve my image, attitude, level of knowledge, or communication skills.

- *Be open for other's creativity.* One of the most important attributes one can have is the ability to stand back and assess a situation or person as if you were a third party, where emotions and pre-existing opinions are set aside long enough to determine what is good for growth and what should be changed or removed.

- *Sharing and caring.* We can share difficult situations when it is relevant to the topic at hand or when it can offer the listener a measure of encouragement or a positive educational lesson. However, consistently talking about your own personal failures or complaints as the main topic of every conversation will not benefit anyone. Everyone should also have a kind and sensitive ear when a family member, friend, or associate truly needs a caring and supportive listener.

- *Envy.* When we see others achieving a level of success that we are still desiring to reach, rise to the occasion and congratulate them for their success. Displaying hard feelings, resentment, or envy can create an unpleasant wedge in relationships. This is not often easy but makes us a valuable friend or co-worker.
- *Negative silent signals.* As 55 percent of our communication skills are nonverbal, always consider what is revealed by your *silent* signals—the impression one receives by what you wear, your grooming, body language and demeanor, posture and attitude. Try watching television with the volume off and try to determine what the characters are saying and feeling by their nonverbal signals. It is an interesting, educational experiment.

Thoughts and Behaviors that Rule Our Destiny

Mental: Psychological, rational, intellectual, yet also emotional and spiritual; involving the mind or a mental process, images of happy or sad times, mental power and mental development.

Compass: Your mental GPS, the navigational instrument for finding your range, the extent of (your) capability, to comprehend the meaning of something.

Destination: The place designated as your journey's end, the ultimate goal for which something is done, (your) life's target.

What key habits and choices create the biggest difference that separates us from the rest of the world?

Achievement-oriented thinkers bring to life the next-level version of themselves mentally first, before they actually arrive at their new destination. What does your own version of a successful you epitomize? How would you think, act, and reveal yourself in this world? Possibly as an excellent life-transforming teacher, highly skilled maintenance technician, gifted technical mind, sensitive caregiver. Adopt the positive characteristics you see in others that pertain to the kind of parent, worker, and so forth that you want to be.

How would you approach your clients who have an indispensable reputation by the way they work, invest in themselves, and believe in themselves? As you see yourself in your desired state of life, career, and relationships, gradually begin to demonstrate your new characteristics, behaviors, and attitudes. Eventually, your actions and outlook will catch up to your thoughts, and you become the successful individual doing what you were meant to do and be. You, not who someone else wanted you to be by vicariously living through you.

Example: If you want to be a high-school teacher and coach, what characteristics would you need to *have?* Strength, self-respect, sense of humor, excellent listening and feedback skills, training in negotiations and problem resolution, care and consideration, being able to differentiate between constructive and destructive criticism. Also, it is important to set yourself apart by how you dress, speak, and communicate. Then, people will want to follow you.

- You live a life with non-negotiable goals and behaviors. As you have assessed what works (listed previously) and what does not (negative behaviors, fear, defeat), you are then be able to release the attitudes and behaviors that do not serve you. These could be ones like, "No, I am not spending several nights a week at the bar" or "I am no longer going to associate with friends who have no motivation in life to get beyond where they are now."
- You *know* you are *worthy of success and ask for what you want.* Yes, ask!
- You are *not* worried about what others think nor do you make your decisions according to whether others approve. Be who you were meant to be, not what someone else wants. *You be you* and they must be themselves.
- When you fail (and everyone does), just know that it puts you one step closer to your goal. Remember Thomas Edison *failed* 1,000 times before he successfully invented the light bulb. He was actively competing with other scientists at the time. The key to success is in not focusing on *failing* but on using each experience as a learning tool, taking what works and throwing out what did not, then moving on! Consider them powerful educational lessons.

- Take action whether you are completely ready or not. Do it afraid if necessary while you actively visualize being in your winner's circle, whether in sports, as a business owner, teacher of the year, award-winning scientist, whatever you were meant to be. No matter what position you hold, you were created to be great! Learn as you go while positioning one foot in front of the other. Choose your steps wisely. Remember, even a job you do not like will teach you lessons for your next rung up the ladder if you let them. As you mentally map your future, do you see any steps that could sidetrack you? Make a list of pros, cons, obstacles, and benefits so your mental GPS is on the fast track.

Whether you think you can or you think you can't, either way you are right!

—Henry Ford

In order to keep a positive mental attitude, you must:

- Carefully assess how many other influences and influencers are in your life (stressors, fun, business and personal contacts, and personality types). What experiences are happening in your career, family, friends, associates, and organizations? What type of behaviors and attitudes do you believe you must emulate to be more successful? Although we must accept that all people have their own set of thoughts and opinions, it is imperative to determine which ones are helping enhance our lives and which ones waste our time with negative influence and which ones hold solid partnerships. Others can positively influence us, but we cannot make anyone else actually change unless they so desire. However, in order to get along with them and not allow their negative attitudes to sway you in your thoughts, accept them for who they are, and expect them to accept you for who you are. If they choose not to be *in your corner* for the good, continue on without them to your chosen purpose.
- Condition your mind each morning to keep it positive under any circumstance. When starting out your day, review any

possible negative people or incidences and rehearse how you will respond in a strong and clear-cut manner. This is so strengthening.

- Steer conversations with others to informative, engaging, and concerned topics. Stop other unfavorable or unproductive conversations in their tracks.
- Make a conscientious effort to praise and give sincere positive comments to those around you. Doing so helps attract more solid people to you in return.
- Always consider what you can offer to alleviate a negative situation or smooth over an injustice. However, focus forward at all times.

You cannot tailor-make the situations in life, but you can tailor-make the attitudes to fit those situations.

—Zig Ziglar

As we can train our minds to focus on the negative, *we can also reprogram our fascinating mental machinery* to leave those self-defeating memories and circumstances behind and focus on the positive. It all depends on what we consciously *choose* to meditate on!

How do success-driven minds think?
Life isn't about finding yourself. Life is about creating yourself.

—George Bernard Shaw

CHAPTER 3

Enter the Winner's Circle Through Brain-Jitsu and a Resilient Human Spirit

Unlock your inner architect. Reprogram Your Mind. Don't deny yourself, develop yourself. The one who has the most power to change your life is the one you see in your mirror!

Research shows that 80 percent of our thoughts are negative. The one most responsible for the outcome of your life is you! Self-esteem is a state of mind and has a powerful hold on your emotions: happy, sad, afraid of failure, confident, determined, or a myriad of feelings that govern what actions you take. What happens when you feel afraid? Do you rise up in anger or back away quickly? Happy? Hug the one next to you? Call everyone who will celebrate with you? Run around the room in a victory lap? When you feel a shot of determination, do you sign up for a class you want to take? Tell someone *No* who wants to distract you? Feel strong inside? A healthy self-esteem is the number one key ingredient to achieving your goals, despite what the world may throw at you at any given time!

- What are your limiting beliefs around the career you truly want and deserve? Yes, *deserve*!
- What are your limiting beliefs that may be keeping you from the relationships you deserve?
- What limiting beliefs are keeping you in a pattern of just barely getting by?
- List the top three limiting beliefs you want to let go of now!

1. _____

2. _____

3._____

First step I must take _____

Second step _____

Third step_____

What positive choices am I replacing these limiting beliefs with? Deciding what to replace them with is critical.

1. _____

2. _____

3. _____

Write a New Program for Your Mind

It truly is never too late for a new beginning where failures and self-sabotage have been kicked to the curb. Hit the Reset Button and launch yourself into the more orderly life you deserve.

The extent to which you can allow yourself to transform is the extent to which you can attract new things without struggle, whether new experiences, new feelings, new people, and more money. Focus on these life- and self-esteem-transforming quotes from victorious overcomers like these:

- *When you embrace those things in you that you do not like, they can no longer hold you hostage.* Author unknown
- *Imagination is everything; it is a preview of life's coming attractions.* Albert Einstein
- *Should you find yourself in a chronically leaking boat, energy devoted to <u>changing</u> vessels* (people, places, things) *is likely to be more productive than energy devoted to patching leaks* (continuing to try to fix the same thing over and over again). Warren Buffett

- *Do just once what others say you cannot do, and you will never pay attention to their limitations again.* James R. Cook 1728–1779, Naval Explorer
- *In the long run, you hit only what you aim at.* Henry David Thoreau, Writer, Philosopher
- *Now is no time to think of what you do not have. Think of what you can do with what there is.* Ernest Hemingway, 1898–1961, American Writer
- *Right now, you are one choice away from a new beginning.* Oprah Winfrey
- *Most great people have achieved their greatest success just one step beyond their greatest failure.* Napoleon Hill
- *A winner is someone who recognizes his God-given talents, works his tail off to develop them into skills, and uses those skills to accomplish his goals.* Larry Bird, Basketball Star
- *You can't change what's going on around you until you change what is going on within you.* Author unknown.

Although you need to associate with positive individuals to help keep self-esteem intact, never allow anyone's opinions to determine what you accomplish or what your value is. Learn from the Queen in Alice in Wonderland: Alice laughed. *"There's no use trying,"* she said. *"One can't believe impossible things. I daresay you haven't had much practice,"* said the Queen. *"When I was your age, I always did it for half-an-hour a day. Why, sometimes I've believed for as many as six impossible things before breakfast"* Lewis Carroll.

Choose a life full of vitality, strength, and positive determination in the midst of our ever-changing world.

Although most people who follow a pattern of lifestyle disarray have an unwitting tendency to thrive on the drama, they find that focusing on the drama relieves them of the necessity of looking inward and taking responsibility for their life choices. Also, they have a tendency to always be a casualty in their life stories. It is time to follow the queen.

Another factor that is often present in a hectic life is feeling guilt. The guilt of not being able to do it all, of having lost something or someone. As you just read, you are one step away from a new beginning. Go!

Questions to Ask Yourself that Indicate You Are Indispensable

Think about how the following traits affect you and those you interact with:

- *Character or temperament:* Your mental and emotional makeup, charm, charisma, appeal. What do others see? Go deep with this. Compare temperament (what you are born with) to computer hardware and your personality to software. Would a few new parts or updated software be just what the doctor ordered? We can change habits with work and obtaining whatever help is needed. A study of your own traits as well as those you are around is very beneficial, including Myers Briggs, or the expanded version, Keirsey Four Points. These provide an excellent understanding of not only what makes *you tick* but how to best communicate with those of different temperaments.
- *Emotion*: Can you interject excitement, passion, and a sense of accomplishment in others? Get to know them, and watch their reactions to your words and actions. Watch how they react to others as well.
- *Core* (of our being): Is your *center* steadfast on making the most of your life and those who are there alongside of you, or does sensory overload have your heart and mind scattered? Carefully strategize what distractions can be eliminated. These include rowdy friends and family, intrusive co-workers, people always asking for favors.
- *Sentiment*: What is your outlook on where you are currently and where others are, or should be? Where can you get new training, help, or motivation to take the necessary steps forward? These include a school counselor, organizational

leader, parent, religious leader, relative, caring neighbor, or someone you know is a respected expert you met in person or online.

- *Mood*: Temper, attitude, disposition, frame of mind. Good, bad, happy, or sad. How is it affecting your relationships, your attitude, and drive? Mood can make us or break us. It can bring people together or cause them to seek conversation elsewhere. Sometimes, just taking a deep breath or two and putting a smile on your face can change your mood and those around you.
- *Mind or intellect*: Attention, concentration, awareness, observance, opinion, conviction. What does your mind spend most of its time and attention on? That is what determines the direction your life will go.
- *Soul*: Will, consciousness, emotions. This is usually where most of our decisions come from, down in our soul. A strong will can be a good thing or also cause problems. Think about how you have experienced this in your own life.
- *Spirit*: Courage, force, determination. The most resilient phenomenon in the universe is the human spirit! Your spirit has unlimited power. Seek out stories of courage and determination. These include an armless woman who drives a car and takes care of her baby with her feet. You will find piano and guitar players who play beautifully with their toes. A woman whose arm had been amputated at her shoulder, making it impossible for a prosthesis, plays the violin in breathtaking fashion. Several with no arms or legs who have become international inspirational speakers because of not letting anything take away their spirit!

Take at least 10 minutes in the morning to visualize and *see* yourself being and doing those very things you desire and need to create in order to fulfill your vision. If you can do this upon awakening when your mind is fresh and you have not yet begun the day with family and job duties, that works best. Writing in a notebook by hand helps you get away from the computer and just focus without distractions. It actually feels good.

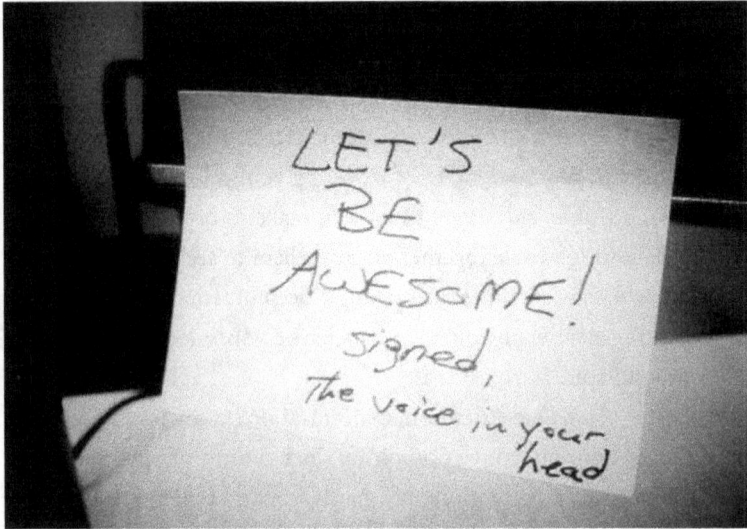

Figure 3.1 **Note:** *Awesome*

If you only have a quiet space in the bathroom with the door locked to fill out your assessment, do it there. Use more paper as necessary to write everything down for weekly review. You can eventually create a blueprint that transforms your mind and alters your everyday life. During this mind transformation time, do not sabotage your efforts by wondering *how* it can come about. Only visualize, visualize, visualize! Behaviors follow.

The majority of people live in *reverse belief,* which explains why there is poverty, illness, fear, hatred, envy, failure, defeat. Positive faith and belief is the common denominator in every successful person. How many times have you given something up and then looked back and wondered whether you gave up too soon? Never again.

Universal Force of Habit: Unwavering Action Steps

The habits we develop and follow from an early age direct us to success or failure, disappointment, or fulfillment. Those patterns are like seeds that continue reproducing the same results, and we continue to attract the same over and over again. Just as the saying goes, "He who aims at nothing shall surely hit it every time." True? Absolutely!

Is there a mental chess game going on when it comes to people pleasers? We all want to be positive influencers, and sometimes, particularly if we lack confidence, we may feel it necessary to do things for others so that they will not think we are inferior. This includes saying *yes* to doing things for others, even though we really do not have the time, energy, or desire, or because we do not want to disappoint or upset them. If we are constantly seeking approval from others in order to be looked upon as a good, indispensable, hardworking, and caring person, we may end up running ourselves ragged and lead from the wrong motives, second-guessing ourselves. Stand firm with a polite *no* when it takes away from what you need to do.

High stress levels have been traced to a national trend toward controlling behavior. Controlling people concern themselves not only with their own thoughts and actions, but insist others think and act in a certain way as well. This is a losing battle, as there is usually more than one approach to doing things. How open are you to exploring new ideas from others? When someone feels worthy of having their idea *considered*, they work harder and take more ownership in their work, relationships, and products.

A study at Massachusetts Institute of Technology (MIT) conveys that:

When it comes to the brain or the neuro processing side of a positive attitude, we now know that a single positive thought causes our brains to produce a chemical electrical signal that affects every cell in our body and transmits at a frequency to the entire quantum field of intelligence. The result? That *energy* goes out to everyone around us. It matters more than we realize what kind of energy and attitude others are picking up on. Every time you are speaking with someone, silently stop and think what kind of energy is emanating from you.

When we have a negative thought, we are releasing negative charges and chemicals in our bodies, and all of that is released through that wide-ranging energy field. Research shows that 80 percent of our thoughts are negative, and that we are the one most responsible for the outcome of those thoughts. Self-esteem is a state of mind and has a powerful hold on our emotions: happy, sad, afraid of failure, confident, determined, or a myriad of feelings that govern what actions we take. A healthy self-esteem

TECHNICAL DIFFICULTIES

REPAIRS UNDERWAY

Figure 3.2 Brain—technical difficulties

is the number one key ingredient to achieving your goals in spite of what the world may throw at you at any given time!

Creative Vision: Building Blocks of All Successful Plans

You can use the human mind to accomplish what others think is impossible just like the examples you previously read about.

- *Manmade vision*: Putting together an idea, items, thoughts, and materials familiar to your mind and using your talents, education, and whatever sources you have available to achieve your goal.
- *Imaginative vision*: This one goes beyond the five senses of sight, smell, hearing, touch, and taste. Imagination operates like a sixth sense. Leonardo da Vinci, Albert Einstein, Walt Disney, Alexander Graham Bell, and Thomas Edison were geniuses in using their creative, imaginative vision to create powerful, life-transforming inventions.

Be assured that *you* too can use your creative mind to get what you want, no matter what others think, do, or say to discourage you! Never stop envisioning the incredible solutions you can design.

Hit the Reset Button! Your Mental GPS Can Transform Your Life, No Matter What!

Here is just one amazing example of a life that went from international success to drastic disaster and back to a happy and accomplished life again: Ted Henter had a promising career as an international motorcycle racer and was world champion numerous times. He became blind in a terrible car accident in 1978, which put an end to his beloved racing career. Ted decided that loss of his eyesight at age 27 was not going to keep him down and out. He became an American computer programmer and businessman who started his own business in 1987. He later invented JAWS, a screen reader for personal computers using MS DOS and later Microsoft Windows. After becoming completely blind, Henter rediscovered waterskiing and started competing in waterskiing competitions. He won six times out of seven competitions in the United States and two internationally. He retired in 1991 after winning the overall gold medal in the United States and World Championship for Disabled Skiers. This is a powerful example of setting your mental GPS for a whole new and successful direction even after a devastating loss!

I once read that no material in the world is as resilient as the human spirit. However, every word and deed can affect that spirit. Relationships impact us immediately from the moment we are born, and some experts say even from within the womb. What happens as we grow up can have a profound effect on our success in life, the patterns we form and live by, and how well we manage the major and minor transitions in life. This basically covers everything we are and do. Now is the time where excuses are no longer accepted and where we realize that no matter what has transpired in our lives, we *can* move forward and live fulfilling and rewarding lives. We can embrace solid relationships that last throughout the rest of our lives. Think of the human spirit as a tire that can get low on air. If it is going flat, pump it back up with positive and constructive thoughts, associations, and growth, then get back on the ride of your life!

If you don't like the hand you have been dealt in the game of life, create a new game!!!

The Three Es of the Road to Success: Enthusiasm, Eagerness, and Excitement

All human brains transmit and receive signals—emotions, attitudes, real or false images, and perceptions. You give off a certain energy when happy, which can draw other positive individuals to you, as it makes them feel good to be around you. The same goes for anger, sadness, strength, and all other types of energy. People can be drawn to it or pushed away by it.

You can build quite a reputation for being kind and understanding or indifferent and uncaring. This will attract or repel individuals at work, home, in social environments, and everywhere you go. How do you feel when someone has just suffered the loss of a loved one or is angry at getting passed over for a promotion they deserved? You can choose to be strong, firm if needed, but still compassionate at the experiences of other human beings. Enthusiasm and empathy are traits that all successful individuals can attain.

Enthusiasm is expressed through our conduct as well as our words. Think of times when something small in significance or status, when expressed with enthusiasm, brought about a partnership, a sale or a new friend. I remember when a well-dressed couple came into the doctor's office with such an impressive presence and great enthusiasm that everyone crowded around and just beamed, so eager to see what they brought. What in the world, I wondered, were they *selling*? Chocolates! Not a miracle medical drug, but chocolates!

The chance of getting what you want, whether of a material, monetary, or emotional nature, is greatly enhanced by the amount of enthusiasm and excitement others perceive you have for your product or service. Just like the chocolate aficionados, you can build a positive mental attitude that can open amazing doors for you collectively in your physical, mental, and social world.

The Art of Self-Discipline and Its Powerful Transforming Capability

- Everything we say affects (whether good or bad) everyone who hears it. Before speaking, always think of your intended goal as well as how your words could be perceived.

- Consider what benefit an argument would have on all involved. Arguing or condemning another person can cause a divide that should be avoided. Active listening and stepping into the other person's shoes can usually give us a much better perspective. Does the issue really even matter enough in the long run to argue or condemn?

How Mental Attitude Affects Personalities

Keeping a flexible, positive mental attitude can be achieved so that the comments or actions of others cannot take control of your day or most certainly of your life. You cannot control what others say and do; however, you can control how you react to it. Determine to always be in tune to how successful people do not get drawn into other people's attitudes or actions. One way is if you know a conversation is coming up that will negatively affect your job, health, reputation, or self-esteem, then prepare mentally ahead of time by rehearsing the scene. Think about the issue at hand, what stance you believe they will take, and what they may say. If you are having a discussion in person, watch their body language for clues: sadness, fear, anger, and hostility, warmth, and so on. List any key points they will possibly bring up. See yourself with controlled posture and confidence in your body signals as well as your voice. What are the most effective words, scenarios, and ultimate problem resolution you can provide to help quell the situation without getting into a confrontation or damaging both your self-image and theirs? Is a session of brain-Jitsu in order? Flip it!

CHAPTER 4

Perception Is Reality: Effectively Communicating With Anyone

In today's global economy, good manners, proper speech patterns, careful grooming, and professional communication skills can make the difference between getting ahead and being left behind. These skills greatly impact your ability to receive the promotion you deserve rather than watching it being given to a less-qualified or less-deserving person. Although it is often not fair, the fact is, even in business relationships, we still judge people by how they act, speak, look, and write. This is particularly true when we are considering partnering with someone to represent us or our company. Our professional manner, communication skills, and attitude wield a powerful influence over their decisions to create a partnership with us, and purchase our products and services.

Why We Seriously Want Good Business Etiquette?

- It makes people want to know us better!
- It differentiates us from all of the competitors who do not practice good business manners.
- It is often the defining reason one person is chosen over another.
- It modifies distracting behaviors that could keep someone from taking us seriously because they are too occupied with our grooming, unfavorable behavior, poor language skills, and so on.

All forms of communications affect others, whether clients, colleagues, suppliers, or friends. The winner may very well be the one with that extra bit of vitality, integrity, and professional appearance. The salesperson who makes an impeccable impression at the table, on the phone, on sales calls, and even online is often the one to seal the deal. Opportunities are lost due to lack of soft skills, even when technical skills are superb. That is why, even technical people are being sent to professional protocol classes to help them better relate to, and communicate clearly and comfortably with, the rest of the business world.

Particularly in industries that handle their money and important business transactions, if we do not *look* the part, we will not *get* the part!

With first-class manners, we also have the advantage of *psychological power* in how others treat us. How? It goes back to that topic of perception. Reflect on how you would respond to a well-groomed, energetic, mannerly, and confident individual versus one who looks disheveled, disorganized, and has poor speech patterns or negative body language. Research has shown time and time again that when two people have similar qualifications, the one who is more polished and professional will almost always be the one chosen for the job or assignment!

The Polished Professional: ?

Figure 4.1 Polished professional

Why is good business etiquette important? Because it differentiates you from the competition and is often the defining reason one person is chosen over another! It makes people want to know you better and have you on their team.

In the working world, your level of self-esteem plays a crucial role in having the career you truly want. Self-image affects not only your ability to get ahead in the working world, but in how well you get along in your personal relationships and with those you come into contact with every day.

Did you know it takes only seven seconds to capture someone's attention? It also takes only 20 seconds to verbally transmit the substance of your message to someone before they decide if they want to listen further or walk away. Although it really is not fair, in the first seven seconds, people are making judgments about our self-image, outlook on life, moral character, economic and educational levels, trustworthiness, social position, and future success. That is hard to believe but true and often happens before even a single word is spoken.

Exceptional business protocol is the epitome of professionalism and is all about presenting ourselves with the kind of presence that shows we can be taken seriously. It is using a code of behavior based on consideration and thoughtfulness. It is treating *all* people with respect, courtesy, manners, and appreciation, no matter who they are or what position they hold.

Professional protocol enables us to have confidence in a *variety* of settings with people from all walks of life. Respect is critical for a solid reputation, one that continually attracts new business and maintains longstanding relationships. Proper protocol also enhances our credibility on sales calls, in negotiations, on the golf course, and definitely while conducting business over meals. What happens during business social events can definitely be a deal maker or deal breaker depending on the perceptions people have of us. Are your manners, appearance, and conversation conducive to building a solid future with others who you want to associate with?

You cannot change your destination *overnight but you can change your* direction *overnight. "Later" is a dream killer. Think about creating your own growth plan.*

—Jim Rohn

Success Starts on the Inside With a Self-Image Checkup

What does self-image have to do with your success? Everything! In the working world, your level of self-esteem plays a crucial part in having the career you truly want. What is self-image? It is how you see yourself, how you believe others see you, and how you allow yourself to be treated. Self-image affects not only your ability to get ahead in the working world, but how well you get along with your family and those you come into contact with every day. Your goal is to make the clearest, most concise, and confident impression possible.

Voice Impressions

Your voice reflects how you are doing and how you feel about your company, your performance, and the business at hand. Exude a positive, energetic attitude. If you feel tired while on the phone, stand up to get your blood flowing during the conversation. Follow cues from the other person. If they are all business and no-nonsense, you should be too. How a person *feels* during communication can greatly impact whether they actually initiate business, follow your lead or whether they are prompted to find some else who will make them feel that they are an important, valued individual. Do they sound professional and interested rather than unfriendly or rushed? Showing engaged interest in them can bring them back around. This includes interested eye contact, leaning in slightly when they are expressing a thought, and active listening where you use a few of their words in your response so they know you *heard* them.

> The most important thing a person can wear is confidence! Confident assurance about who he or she is—poised, secure, and positive in spite of what is going on in life!

First Step, a Self-Image Checkup

What does your self-image have to do with opening the door to new opportunities? Everything! In society as a whole, and in the working world, your level of self-esteem and your self-image play a crucial role in having the kind of career and relationships you truly want and deserve.

What is self-image? It is
(1) how you see yourself ("as a man thinks in his heart, so is he")
(2) how you believe others see you
(3) how you allow yourself to be treated

Self-image affects not only your ability to get ahead in the working world, but how you get along with your family and those you come into contact with every day. It is one of life's most important ingredients, giving you the ability to move forward in life with confidence, know that you deserve good things, and that you are absolutely *more than enough*. It makes you smile and helps you meet the challenges of life head on.

We often limit our success by our self-perception. This includes the way we think, how we interpret ourselves and the world based on our past experiences. If we expect rejection, failure, and discouragement, due to prior encounters, previous conditioning, and self-talk, that is what comes knocking on our door. If we anticipate greater success, satisfying personal and professional relationships, or becoming a successful entrepreneur, then our energy and focus are like a magnet taking us toward those goals. Unfortunately, some individuals follow the same format of defeat for a lifetime, unable to still reach their goal because they were not able to in the past. Why? There are any number of reasons, such as a myriad of personal struggles, lack of finances, limited education, their own personality traits, or the people closest to them causing hindrances by their words or treatment.

I'm a determined winner!!!   I'm a dysfunctional failure!

Figure 4.2 Perception is reality

Many individuals have faced the additional challenge of feeling like they never fit in, or have only heard discouraging words from parents, teachers, or others who have been a key part of their life. The list of characteristics and circumstances is limitless. If that is you, go back to that list of successes who were initially told they would never amount to anything. They went amazingly far though, did they not?

Our perceptions may be correct; however, they are often partially or completely false. How many opportunities do we miss because we do not perceive ourselves as good enough, competent enough, educated enough, or dressed nicely enough? We can fill in the blank with any number of reasons. Let us show the world that we are smart, experienced, professional, and look the part of someone who knows where he or she is going and what plans are needed to get there! As some of the most successful people have said, "Fake it until you make it!" There is a lot of wisdom in there!!

Your new motto: Step aside world, I'm coming through!

Your Personal Branding Checklist

Quality networking events can help land a wealth of new contacts, prospects, and clients. How can we come across as the confident professional who provides the kind of products and services they want? As we definitely need more than a 30-second elevator pitch and a list of services to push at them, the following are additional success tips to keep you on the cutting edge:

1. *Arrive on time, with erect and friendly posture,* to avoid being rushed, disheveled, or preoccupied. That way, the maximum amount of quality interactions can be made in the short period of time that most events last. This can be difficult for individuals who are shy or who do not want to be there in the first place. It is, however, part of the process of growing our professional brand, networking skills, and number of clients or customers.

2. *Get your smile on and move!* Shy, introverted personalities network more easily when deciding ahead of time how many people to meet

before arriving. Set a reasonable goal, possibly 8–10 new people, then get the ball rolling. Just a simple "Hello, how are you? What brings you here today?" can start a conversation. "What types of businesses, services, or people are you interested in meeting?" will definitely get them interested in talking to you about what *they* want from the meeting. Before moving to the next person, ask who they know that could also use your products and services. By all means, reciprocate and connect them with others you know who could use their services as well.

3. *Adhere to the one-minute rule.* Let the other person talk at least 60 percent of the time. Avoid the risk of losing their attention by conducting a long-winded monologue. Dominating a conversation does not make for a successful sale or relationship, only for causing people to do an about face and move on.

4. *Less is more!* There is no need to work the entire room! When an individual bounces from person to person, slipping a business card into any available hand, those receiving the cards feel as if they are just part of an assembly line. Take the time to truly connect with a few individuals rather than quickly running around the room making a fast sales pitch. If there is someone standing close by whom you know, be sure to introduce both parties to each other. They will appreciate the fact that you care about them and are not just trying to add names to their potential client list.

Following is a checklist to use until these habits become second nature. Record your thoughts on each point. What can you do to make your professional image even better?

- Stand in front of a full-length mirror before leaving home and take a close look at your appearance. It is the only way to be sure that the look you have achieved is the one you want to project to the world. Are there any areas that need improvement? What have you seen others wear to those types of events?

- Clothes reflect your personality and commitment to doing a good job. Are they simple, tailored to your particular industry,

and attractive without being distracting? What is the message
you are projecting? Does it say you are serious yet friendly
and professional, or does it say you are totally thinking about
meeting friends after work for drinks?

- Is your hairstyle flattering to your facial shape and business
  you are in?
- Are accessories understated and attractive (not flashy, clank-
  ing, sparkly if in a conservative position) so that they do not
  look more appropriate for partying than for the workplace?
  Switching out pieces of clothing or accessories for other events
  after work is much more favorable.
- How is your voice? Record it for a day or two and then
  listen to yourself. Is it strong and clear, or is there a nasal
  sound? Does it have a deep, rich quality or sound high-
  pitched, thin or weak? Would you like to listen to this
  voice? If the answer is no, practice controlling your pitch,
  rate, tone, and overall voice quality until the answer is yes.
  Watch characters on television to see what impressions they
  make and what a strong, weak, caring, or sarcastic tone
  sounds like. Practice in the mirror or on your cellphone
  to play back.

Communication Skills that Make You (Not Break You)!

As it only takes approximately 20 seconds to get beyond the initial visual
and verbal messages before determining if someone wants to continue the
conversation, it is important to have a quick and interesting introduction
that projects energy and tells them what you do and the services you provide. An example would be, "I provide individuals who want to change
careers with new thought processes and communication techniques to
greatly enhance their marketability." Check their reaction and demeanor.
Then add, "Thank you for asking, and would you please share with me
what do you do?"

Mingling: How Do We Network Effectively?

Figure 4.3 Networking

Temper greetings. Americans love handshakes and being on a first-name basis. Other cultures have their own methods of greeting, such as bowing in Japan. If a guest is from a different ethnic background, learn proper greetings for his or her native customs and use them. If possible, use a few polite words of greeting in their national language. Titles, rank, and status are very important to them, so do not use their first name until invited to do so. Listen carefully to their introduction, engage them in a comfortable conversation, and be in tune with who they are and what they do.

Why Is It So Difficult to Remember Someone's Name?

During the first few moments of meeting someone, we are checking them out visually, looking at their clothing, hair, grooming, demeanor, or a myriad of other things, before we actually start *listening*. Because of that, we are not really *hearing* them!

The best way to introduce yourself, particularly when in a room where each person stands up at their table to introduce themselves is to say

(1) what you do, (2) for whom, (3) your name. By the time they hear your name, they have shifted from your outer appearance to your verbal message. Scan the room as you speak, keeping within the set time limit for each person to give their very quick introduction. Listen carefully for those who have the type of personality and business you want to associate with. Connecting is for a quick assessment, not to conduct business. Set up an appointment for coffee, lunch, or an in-house meeting to further your conversation.

Attending an Event but Not Sure What the Dress Code Is?

We always want to stand out as a quality professional and not be remembered for our clothing. To be on the safe side, put another shirt or blouse—dressier or more casual, an extra pair of shoes and socks (lightweight socks go with lighter weight shoes), and possibly a different jacket and accessories in the car. If you notice others dressed quite differently, slip into a bathroom and make a quick change. The same goes for casual, business-related outings. Pressed shorts and clean sneakers make a much better impression than a tee shirt with the Grateful Dead's last nationwide tour on it along with cut-off shorts and old sneakers. Now, go in with confidence and impress them with your fantastic personality!!! Perform some brain jujitsu if need be. Rock it!!

Business Cards

Many important business deals are conducted during functions outside of the 8–5 world. Doing business within a global economy requires that we pay attention to other customs and protocol, including our professional calling cards. Particularly, in international circles, business cards explain our place in the corporate hierarchy, so our title should be clearly stated. Have plenty of cards but be choosy about giving them out to everyone in the room as unsolicited cards will usually go into the *circular file* in short order. Always offer your card facing *them*, so they can immediately read it.

Of course, a business card should identify *you*, but also enable you to stand out from the crowd. If part of a corporation, you must abide by their

Very unique. Usually, two different type of fonts is best but no more than three. You would certainly remember this card, right?

Be careful that there is not so much color, text and photos that the person's eyes are shifting all over the place to find your contact information.

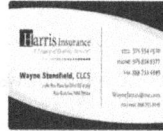

Excellent example of showing the reader exactly what you do!

Standard, easy-to-read format for a product or service where all employees must have a consistent image.

Figure 4.4 Business cards

standard design; however, if you own a business, you have the opportunity to reflect your personality on the business card and marketing materials. It may be beneficial to include other important information in addition to phone numbers and an e-mail address. If you have a website, Facebook, Twitter, LinkedIn, or YouTube sites, you may include them on the back.

There are different schools of thought regarding having a picture on one's business card. Many companies have a standard design that does not allow for a photo. If in sales, real estate, service organizations, or other competitive markets, a photo can distinguish you from your competitors and help everyone remember you much easier. Investigate what other successful individuals in your industry are doing.

If the company allows a photo, get a professional one that depicts the type of business you do or clients you want. This is a very good way to remember the face with the name for a later meeting.

> Canva and VistaPrint are two excellent sources for designs you can create through their vast array of templates. They are high quality, and the finished product quickly shows up at your door. You can also view Fiverr to find a talented individual to create marketing materials for you.

Following are valid reasons to exchange cards when the individual is:

- A *potential* client, buyer, or supplier
- A link to a colleague, former classmate, business owner, or co-worker

- Someone you would like to know on a social or community level
- Someone who is willing to pass your card on to another individual
- Someone who needs or wants your updated information (title, phone number, and so on)
- Someone who shows genuine interest in getting to know you, your products, or business even better

Image and Good Manners Make the Difference

Our self-image, behaviors, and abilities are relayed to those around us through communication skills that are broken down into three parts:

- 55 percent of our message is nonverbal: how we look, act, sit, stand, enter a room, our posture, movements and gestures, handshake, what we do with our hands and eyes, facial expressions, how high we hold our head, and so on
- 38 percent is the quality of voice: our verbal expressions, pitch, and tone (friendly, annoyed or irritated, dismissive, supportive, and so on)
- Only 7 percent are the actual words we speak

Whether we meet someone for the first time or the tenth, it is critical to project a confident, yet friendly demeanor that says, "I want to build, or continue building, a *mutually rewarding* relationship with you." Remember, we only have one chance to make a good first impression! A positive and confident "presence" makes us more approachable, believable, and appealing to our prospects. However, poor presentation can repel people, giving the impression that we are not as effective or straightforward as they want in a business partner.

Kinesics: the art of reading nonverbal signals helps us *interpret* what others are really saying so we know how to frame our response. Example: if someone is saying something nice but their body is stiff and there is fire in their eyes, it is usually more accurate to believe what the face and demeanor are actually saying rather than just their words. Pay attention to sudden changes in their posture, expression, or other cues because you may have hit a nerve. If they all of a sudden act or speak to you in a different mode, go back and think about what just happened and what might have triggered the change. Ask questions, clarify for agreement (or disagreement), explain yourself again, or change directions in order to get them back on a constructive course. An example is "You look concerned. Tell me what your thoughts are on this." The more you practice this skill, the more effective and favorable relationships you will have.

By watching a job candidate or business prospect's *silent* signals, we can discern how aggressive they may be, whether they come across as obnoxious, personable, are shy, or feel inferior. Bottom line, technical skills are not the only requirement for a new job or business opportunity. Good soft skills are critical for taking us where we want to go in life and in business.

Introductions and Mingling: How Do I Conduct Myself?

The main point in any introduction is to lean slightly forward, give a warm handshake, smile, and be totally sincere and engaged in getting to know *them*. If we can distinguish what color of eyes they have, we have made a solid connection! When shaking hands, maintain a stance of about 18 inches from the other person in order to respect their *individual space*.

Many people are uncomfortable mingling during a networking event. We are often worried about what people will think of us. The easiest way to get around that is to put our focus on *them*. How? First of all, look for people who appear somewhat lonely, standing by themselves. They appreciate us coming up to them and initiating a conversation. That helps get relationship-building conversations started while promoting confidence in ourselves *and* the other person. It is easier to join a group previously engaged in a discussion after someone leaves, breaking the circle of participants, which then allows you to comfortably slip right in. The following guidelines will also help:

- People more readily approach when your back is to light, such as standing in front of a window during the daytime

- Keep your posture erect, palms up with arms and fingers open, and a friendly smile that invites conversation
- Be mindful that the best conversationalists are the ones with the best *listening* skills!

Introductions can be confusing, so here is an easy way to confidently introduce two people:

- Introduce the person with the *least important* title (regardless of gender) to the person with the most important title. For example: Mr. or Ms. Greater Authority, I would like to introduce you to Mr. or Ms. Lesser Authority. An example is saying a company president's name before a sales representative. When introducing someone to an individual from another company, however, the one with the *highest position* is actually the guest, or client … even if he or she holds a *lesser* title.
- Introductions should be brief. "How do you do?" or "Hello" is fine. Always relay the message that "*It* is very nice to meet you" rather than "I am happy to meet you." Stating "I" first puts the emphasis on you rather than them. If you cannot remember someone's name, reintroduce yourself, and they will often say their name again. If they do not, say something like, "We met at last month's marketing conference at the Embassy Suites. I'm (name)." They should offer it to you at that point. If they still do not, just smile and say, "I apologize. May I have your name again please?" The main point to remember is to lean slightly forward with erect posture, give a warm handshake, smile, and be totally sincere and engaged in getting to know *them* and what *they* do!

Conversational Starters

Those you are networking with, or who are attending a party, greatly appreciate a considerate introduction with other attendees. This includes a conversational starter you provide before you move on to others, and they now have an interesting fact to begin their discussion with.

Example: "Dr. Smith, I would like to introduce you to my friend Carol Johnson. Carol, this is Dr. John Smith, head of Internal Medicine at Nebraska Medicine. Carol just moved her from Phoenix." Both first and last name and one fact about each one has been provided.

When Shaking Hands

Women usually offer their hand first, but either gender is welcome to initiate the universal greeting of the handshake. Take the other person's hand with medium pressure, palm to palm, in a vertical hold, and pump two to three times, leaning slightly forward. Watch out for salespeople who were taught to hold your hand horizontally with theirs on top. This is a nonverbal tactic used to subconsciously *have the upper hand* in controlling the direction the conversation will go. Politely turn your hand back to a vertical position and continue shaking hands. They will get the message that you are on a *psychologically* equal-playing field.

Concept of Interaction Zones

Research indicates that group performance is enhanced at closer, face-to-face distances of approximately 18 inches. However, it is important to note that this is *too close* for comfort for some individuals. Generally speaking, men tend to prefer greater distances in communication than women are comfortable with.

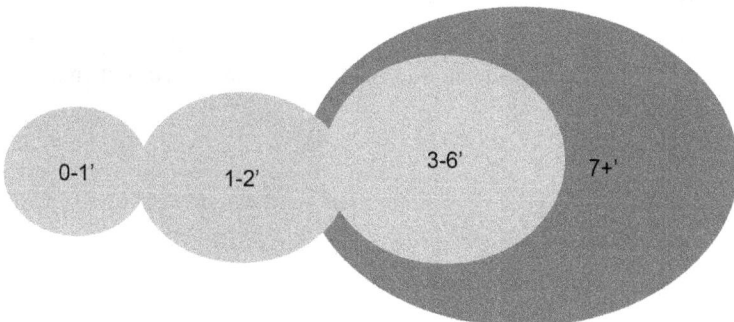

Figure 4.5 Interactive zones

The concept of interaction zones is used to illustrate individuals' preferred zones of physical closeness during communication and interactions. Commonly defined as:

- Public   7 or more feet (examples are walking away from a purse in a grocery cart, bathroom stalls, theater seats)
- Social   3–6 feet (part of a group, not yell to be heard, inner circle)
- Personal   1–2 feet (conversations, closer interactions)
- Intimate   0–1 foot

Exhibit Friendly Bravery

At business social functions, shyness may be misunderstood as being socially unskilled, so try introducing yourself to as many people as possible. Even if you really do not want to be there, stay at least a half hour and make the rounds before leaving. This can keep you in the winner's circle by exhibiting a team player attitude, and it is definitely good for your work relationships.

At business social functions, you are still under scrutiny. Your attire should not be too casual or revealing, as that impression will carry back to the workplace and can affect promotional opportunities. You still want to be remembered as the sharp professional (regardless of your vocation), not for what you wore. One year when I worked for a large computer aggregator, a young woman with a very promising future wore a very low-cut dress complete with large strategically placed rose tattoo to the company Christmas party. Everyone saw the tattoo along with a lot of cleavage. She was never again viewed the same by others as a serious contender for the promotion she was seeking and almost had, but then was passed over for.

- Always hold your glass in your left hand when mingling so the right one is dry and free to shake hands.
- Drink a glass of water or coffee between alcoholic drinks to maintain a sharp, professional conversation at all times. It is better to keep alcoholic beverages to just one during the event.

- To build up your network and acquire new friends and acquaintances, make it a habit to introduce yourself to at least five people you do not know. Always focus on *them*, which also helps if you are *self*-conscious.
- Your date is also under scrutiny. Adults should not introduce someone as *boyfriend* or *girlfriend*. Offer their first and last names and possibly one introductory comment to enable those being introduced to start a conversation. A spouse or fiancé should be introduced as such.
- Always thank the host or hostess and let them know how much you appreciate their hospitality. A handwritten thank you note is a good way to keep a favorable relationship going.
- If you are nervous and have hands that perspire, roll a bit of antiperspirant over your palms before entering the room.
- If you have the nervous problem of your lips getting stuck to your teeth, a thin film of Vaseline on your upper teeth will do the trick.
- At a sit-down meal, follow the host or hostess as to when to put your napkin in your lap and pick up your fork. Observe whether they ask a blessing and sit quietly during this time.

Dress for the position you want, if it is different from what you currently have!

Your wardrobe reflects your personality, including if you are creative, dramatic, intellectual, conservative, unsophisticated, or careless. Avoid wearing clothing that overwhelms your size or personality. You do not want your outfit to speak louder than your own character; however, you may perk up a drab personality by wearing clothing that is more appealing and friendly. Also, be sure to replace poor-quality belts and buttons to add more value and sophistication to your clothing. Anything with belt loops *must* be worn with a belt or cut the loops off.

Figure 4.6 Dressing for position

Clothing should help us move up socially and in business, not hold us back! Appearance can work for us by projecting a refined, confident image. It can also work against us by exhibiting scuffed, run-down shoes, wrinkled clothing, unkempt fingernails, or disheveled hair. The latter gives the impression of low self-esteem, carelessness, or that there is no motivation to go any further in life. We always want to be recognized as an accomplished, intelligent, and articulate professional, rather than remembered for what we wore.

How well I remember the gentleman who came into the human resources department of a large corporation where I used to work. He was very qualified as far as his education and work experience, but the hiring manager would not hire him. When I asked her why, she said it was because of the little nubs on his collar where friction can slightly rough up the fabric. In her opinion, he "lacked attention to detail because he did not remove them." Pretty harsh? You bet! Unfortunately, many people will make determinations about our abilities from such seemingly minute details.

Ever been puzzled by how some people react to you when wearing certain types or colors of clothing? Does that red suit seem to irritate your boss every time you wear it? Try a dress for a positive impact calendar! Keep a calendar for at least three weeks, writing down the following before going to bed: What you wore, including color and style or type of outfit. Include how you felt (powerful, professional, not so hot, disorganized), then notate how others treated you (warm, aloof, indifferent, with respect, like you were an authority, friendly—or dismissed you or seemed annoyed). It will not take long before you discover what clothing items you should invest in and what should go to charity. You will discover a pattern emerge of either positive or negative feelings and reactions from others. These responses can help guide you in making any changes needed that will benefit your career. All of the research done throughout the years has proven that it truly does make a difference.

Branding Yourself for Success

Every day, we present our thoughts and ideas to business prospects, teachers, parents, organizations, friends, or even the one in line next to us. Our first interaction will leave a lasting impression, so make it the best one! As 55 percent of our message is nonverbal, make sure your body is relaying the same message as your mouth. Whether you are giving a sales presentation to a large number of individuals, sitting across from two people at a table, or trying to raise funds for a worthy cause, use the following tips to ensure your nonverbal signals bring the success you are aiming for. The more positive and confident your interactions, the greater your success in building a relationship that could last for years. Following are signals that can either enhance or impair your brand:

- *Your energy.* Be aware of the energy you are transmitting! Is it motivating, positive, exciting, confident, worrisome, pre-occupied? Set a positive tone with your facial expressions, sincere eye contact, and friendly, yet controlled, body language. Nonverbal signs of defiance, angst, fear, or frustration could propel the listener to the other side of the room if your words are saying something entirely different from what your body is projecting!

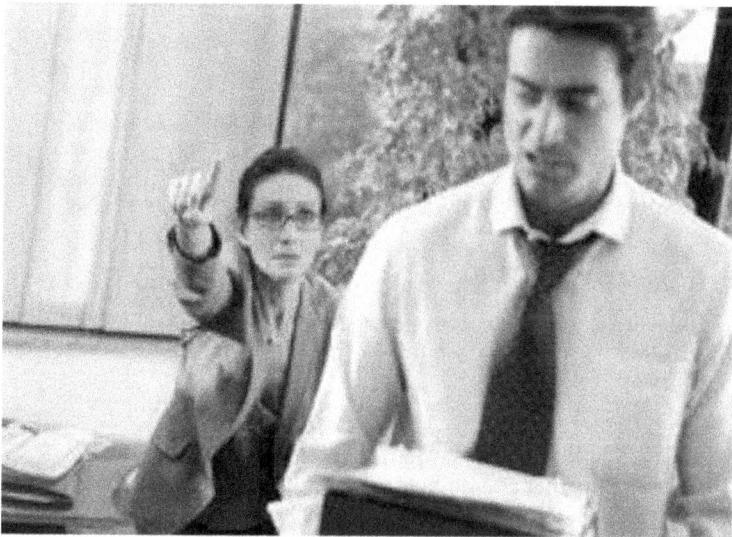

Figure 4.7 Nonverbals

- *Hands.* It is said that eyes and hands are open and closed according to the person's present state of mind. They tell so much about you. As mentioned in the introduction, hands should face them with palms up and fingers open, welcoming them to come into your space, or at your side. If you are new at speaking and feeling uncomfortable, holding (not waving) a pen may help. Having one hand in your pocket briefly is acceptable, but both hands in your pockets gives the impression of either being arrogant, lacking confidence, or hiding something.

- *Eye contact.* In the United States, eye contact is necessary for honest, productive conversations. In some other countries, looking someone in the eye could be considered disrespectful. Good eye contact gives the impression that you are trustworthy, confident, credible, and serious about your conversation or presentation.

- *Your eyes.* Avoid darting eyes, scanning people's shoes, or any eye messages that give the impression you are not completely engaged in a conversation with them.

- *Statements or questions.* When people raise their voices at the end of a statement, it sounds like they are questioning themselves rather than making a statement. The listener may think, "If you are not sure what you are talking about, why should I take you seriously?" Result? You can be overlooked in business meetings, presentations, or as a valuable part of the team. Approximately 80 percent of the voiceovers on television are done by men because their lower pitch lends to their credibility. Soft or high-pitched voices can give the impression of not being capable enough to manage the task as successfully as someone else.

- *Adjust your mode of speaking* according to the type of group you are talking to. Be more energetic if speaking to someone of like manner and do not overwhelm anyone with a boisterous voice if they are quiet and reserved.

- Your goal is to make the clearest, most concise, and confident impression possible.

Success Starts on the Inside, With a Self-Image Checkup

Establish what you can do that is outside of your comfort zone and yet will help grow your business the most. Following are some examples:

- Determine to meet 10 people at the next networking event rather than staying within the comfort of those you already know. Shy people find it very helpful to start attending networking events by offering to help at the registration table or somewhere else at the event, so people notice them first.
- Starting today, find, register for, and attend quality webinars (many of them are free) to help reprogram your mind and teach you new skills for greater success.
- Become active in a few applicable local groups and online social media. Invest in some quiet time in order to take positive steps that will reap noticeable results!

What Does One's Own Perception Have to Do With It Anyway?

Your perception of yourself shapes the perception others will have of you. Your goal is to be perceived as a confident, caring, engaging, and knowledgeable person who sincerely desires to provide the best products, services, and relationships possible.

Positive signals can increase sales, make us more approachable and more believable. Negative signals repel people and give the impression that we may not be an effective businessperson or are not telling the truth. If we use these signals consciously and read what other people are saying, it can help us frame our responses.

A question to ask yourself daily is, "Do I send out the message to others that *I* am the one they want to do business with because *I* am the best?"

Now stop! Take some time to really examine the following points and determine: "What is the most important area that I would like to change as far as the personal and professional persona I am displaying to others?"

- Could it be getting in better shape to appear more energetic and motivated, able to successfully handle their business?
- Could it be working on simple body language changes such as a more confident handshake, erect posture, and engaging eye contact?
- How about changes in grooming to show others that I take good care of myself; therefore, I will also take equally good care of them and their business?
- What would make me be more confident, organized, and ready to take on the big guys? These could include speech class, an image consultant, social media tips, and techniques.
- Consider how your attitude, energy, and appearance are formulating a particular image in the mind of the one you are speaking with.
- What kind of energy are you transmitting? Is it positive, negative, forceful, supportive?
- What have you observed in yourself in the past? Are there patterns you would like to change to bring about new relationships or career opportunities? You would be amazed how a pattern of *it is all about me* can be incredibly powerful when changed to one of confidence, yet with a servant's heart to help improve the lives of others. Many people gravitate to that kind of person with great respect and a desire to be part of their team.
- What can a *trustworthy* close friend or confidante tell you about the energy you are projecting? You read this statement before. Are you watching and *feeling* what messages are projected?

As previously stated, did you ask yourself, "If I were viewing myself from another person's perspective, would I want to do business with me?" Did you clearly determine all of the issues that led you to the *why* or *why not* question? These include if your appearance, manner, and speech exhibit the kind of characteristics that would prompt you to do business with yourself. Do you like what you are seeing?

Networking: Exhibiting the Kind of Impression That You *Want* to Give

When conducting business, including business-related social events, ensure that you are exhibiting the kind of impression that you truly *want* to give to others, especially your competition!

Share interesting stories. Are you comfortable initiating conversations with people you have never met when you are at networking events? How about preparing ahead of time? Gear topics for the kind of people and professions those attending are active in, if possible.

First, do a self-assessment. List what is interesting about you that you can share with others. *Yes*, you *do* have many interesting (business appropriate) things to share! Put pen to paper and begin listing them. Include your passion for writing, fundraising, organizational skills, creativity, coaching, writing, mechanics, and so on. It is not all about *what* you do but *who* you are as a person!

What goal did you accomplish that they may be interested in? These can include hobbies and activities out of the business world as long as the attendees can relate. Many individuals are also very interested in sports,

Figure 4.8 Introductions

arts, music, antiques, public speaking, writing, and so on. Be prepared for some friendly conversation as well as the serious side of your meeting. Practice a few real-life stories ahead of time so that your conversation will flow naturally. Adjust the level of formality depending on who you are talking to, their type of business, and kind of product or service you are offering. Additionally, talking to a mechanic about new equipment requires a different wardrobe and level of formality in speech than meeting the CEO of a financial firm.

What specifically are you are doing, or have done, that will make you interesting? Engaging? Or that validates your experience, knowledge, and why you stand above your competition?

Be as descriptive as possible. For example, which one of these phrases gets your attention? "I sell insurance," or "I share powerful examples of where the insurance plans my clients and I design together are protecting them from a possible misfortune. They are able to attain a comfortable financial cushion for them later on in life." Yes, it is all about them and how you can get them the product or service they want or desire.

Work on the script until it flows, sounds confident, and depicts the true nature of your business and capabilities. As you meet new clients and build new business relationships, be intent on presenting yourself in a positive manner, upbeat, self-assured, and secure about your work and life. Quick testimonies of the benefits others have experienced with your product or service can really make a difference.

Write out and practice introducing yourself to a variety of individuals from various industries. If they are interested in sales, focus more on that. If they are seeking a technical person or maintenance worker, let them know about your specific expertise *after* you clearly hear what they are needing.

While thinking about these newly prepared introductions, assess the results of your interactions after each meeting. How? Once you leave the event, remember how comfortable you were and how others responded to you. Depending on how successful those conversations went, modify your introductions and stories accordingly. Could you ask other attendees more questions about *themselves* and *their* businesses to keep the ball rolling in a more engaging conversation? Next time you meet someone new, first, find out what *they* do.

Bottom line, technical skills are not the only requirement for new or continued business opportunities. Good soft skills are critical for taking you where we want to go in life and in business.

CHAPTER 5

Gain Powerful Credibility Through Engaging Communication and Presentation Skills

Every day, we present our thoughts and ideas to business prospects, teachers, parents, organizations, friends, or even the one in line next to us. Our first interaction will leave a lasting impression, so make it the best one! Whether you are giving a sales presentation to a large number of individuals, sitting across from two people at a table, or trying to raise funds for a worthy cause, use the following tips to ensure your nonverbal signals bring the success you are looking for. The more positive and confident your interactions, the greater your success in building a relationship that could last for years. Following are signals that can either enhance or impair your brand.

Presentation Skills

- *Your energy.* Be aware of the energy you are transmitting! Is it motivating, positive, exciting, confident, worrisome, pre-occupied? Set a positive tone with your facial expressions, sincere eye contact, and friendly, yet controlled body language. Nonverbal signs of defiance, angst, fear, or frustration could propel the listener elsewhere.
- *Eye contact.* In the United States, eye contact is necessary for honest, productive conversations. In some other countries, looking someone in the eye could be considered disrespectful. Good eye contact gives the impression that you

are trustworthy, confident, credible, and serious about your conversation or presentation.

- *Statements or questions.* When people raise their voices at the end of a sentence, it sounds like they are questioning themselves rather than making a statement. The listener may think "If you are not sure what you are talking about, why should I take you seriously?" Result? You can be over-looked in business meetings, presentations, or as a valuable part of the team. Soft or high-pitched voices can cause the speaker to lose credibility by giving the impression of not being capable or able to manage the task as successfully as someone else.
- Always hold a beverage in your *left* hand to avoid a wet and clammy handshake.
  Your goal is to make the clearest, most concise, and confident impression possible.
  Determine what you can do that is outside of your comfort zone and yet will help grow your business the most. Here are some examples:
- Resolve yourself, especially if you are introverted, to meet ten people at the next networking event rather than staying within the comfort of those you already know.
- Starting today, find, register for, and attend quality webinars to help reprogram your mind and teach you new skills for greater success. Many of them are free. Check to see what webinars may include virtual conversations so that you can begin participating while in the comfort of your own private space.
- Become active in a few applicable local groups and active online social media. Search topics that are educational, fun, motivating. Invest in some quiet time in order to take positive steps that will reap noticeable results!

How exceptional telephone skills impact business success! Every phone call represents you and your company. An important part of building good business relationships is giving the impression of being a confident professional that clients and co-workers will be eager to have on their team. Consider the following techniques to help market yourself for greater success:

- *How you sound:* How we sound when answering the phone can influence whether someone chooses to do business with us or not, as poor conduct can sever professional and personal relationships. Callers do not see what is going on at the other end of the phone. How many times have we spoken to someone and heard them typing or shuffling papers? It gives the impression that we are not worthy of their time and attention. Always terminate live conversations before answering a call, take a deep breath, and put a smile on your face! As mentioned earlier, stand up if you need to for a more enthusiastic and interested voice.

- *The impression our voice creates:* Our voice reflects how we are doing and how we feel about our business and theirs. Exude a positive, engaged, energetic attitude. Serious conversations need a firm and confident voice but with a controlled tone. Follow cues from the other person. If they are all business and no-nonsense, we should be too. This includes comments sounding professional and interested, not unfriendly or rushed. How a person *feels* during a call can greatly impact whether they actually initiate business, or whether they are prompted to find someone else who will make them feel that they are an important, valued customer or client.

- *Ending your conversation:* Provide a conclusive statement: "I will get the final figures to you by Friday," or "I agree that we need more research before making a final decision." End the call on a positive note such as, "It was nice talking with you," or "I'm glad we were able to clear up this matter and move forward. Let's meet next week to review our next steps."

Breaking Away from an Awkward Networking Conversation

- Have you ever felt stuck in an awkward conversation at a business networking or social event?
- Although it is necessary to remain polite and professional for the sake of your career and reputation, it is important to have a clear exit strategy in order to move on to constructive and beneficial conversations. Insightful preparation is key to graciously removing yourself from unproductive or unnecessary encounters.

Shift Connections

- The best way to be helpful without using up your time in an unproductive conversation is to discover what the person's needs and interests are and what they hope to accomplish (sales, qualified employee, and so on) from that event. Then, introduce him or her to someone better suited to for their interests or business. This builds trust and a larger network for all involved.
- For instance, if the individual is seeking a new employment opportunity, introduce them to a recruiter or someone who may be seeking a qualified person in a similar industry. After your introduction, smile, tell them you are happy to have made the connection, and excuse yourself to join another person or group.

Dining Etiquette and Business Entertaining

Please note: Most executives have not had the luxury of attending finishing school; however, they are expected to handle business in the dining room as well as they handle it in the boardroom!

Manners are an integral part of business for anyone who wants to achieve and maintain a competitive edge. It is not only the conscious things we do but also the unconscious things (slurping, elbows on the table, tapping fingers, cellphones) during meals that differentiate us, either positively or negatively, from the competition. What is the focus of the meeting?

Interruptions and annoyances: Business deals are not only made at the dining table; they can be broken as well. When looking around in restaurants, how many people do we see talking on their cellphones, while others are sitting there waiting for that individual to get off the phone? At business meals, it is all about *them*! Other than when one is expecting a critical call, cellphones should be completely removed from the table and, at least on vibrate, if not turned off.

- What is your goal? Is it to build a relationship? Make it all about the prospective client or guest. What is happening in your prospect's industry? Discover any details about the meeting companion ahead of time to aid you in asking the most intelligent questions during the meal, coffee, or happy hour.
- Avoid controversial subjects such as politics, religion, or personal matters. Etiquette is about ensuring that those around us are comfortable in our presence.

A Note of Appreciation and Follow-Through

A verbal *thank you* at the end of the meal is appropriate and appreciated, and a handwritten thank you note adds a special touch that can bring you top of mind to the recipient. You are more apt to be invited back again for another discussion and possible business deal when you exhibit good manners.

Develop Successful Rapport

When communicating with others, misunderstandings can take place due to a number of factors such as distractions in the room or preconceived notions others may have about us or our business. *How* we say something may cause the message to be misconstrued by the listener. To enhance confident and professional rapport, watch their reactions while you follow these tips:

Adjust the way you speak according to the type of person you are talking with, that is, strong and outgoing, shy and not very communicative, or

Elbows on the table can only be after a meal where there is engaging conversation.

Figure 5.1 Table talk

one who projects either a positive or negative attitude. Stand taller and speak in a strong voice if the person has a very assertive demeanor and is very outgoing. A lower volume and softer approach work well to avoid overwhelming a shy, quiet person or one who could be intimidated by a more powerful voice and body language.

Am I the best ambassador for my company? How do you score with the following career-enhancing tips?

- Do I always remember that I am acting, officially or unofficially, as my company's public relations representative even when I am off the job? Are my employees, or partners, doing the same?
- How familiar am I with my company's products, services, history, marketing materials, publicity, and other literature? What more can I learn to make me an indispensable part of the company?

Today, determine: What one NEW product, service, outer impression, or dialog can I provide that will be different and will positively impact my business?

CHAPTER 6

Is That Really Me Giving That Confident Presentation?

Are there actually more people in the world who are afraid of speaking in front of others than in dying? Yes, 54 percent of adults are more afraid of public speaking than death! What are we afraid of? Messing up? Being rejected? Feeling foolish? Judgment? Unsure if our audience will think we do not know what we are talking about? Have your normally dry palms become so sweaty you could not even hold onto a football? When you speak, does that upper lip suddenly get stuck to your front teeth? Do you feel like you just swallowed a large walnut?

If you are you among the 54 percent of the adults who are afraid of public speaking, you are missing one of the most powerful ways to market yourself, get your message out, and create new income opportunities! You *can* learn effective techniques to move forward!

Establishing credibility in your presentations includes more than sharing technical knowledge. It is imperative to build trust, conduct engaging rapport with your audience, know your competition's business, and present a confident, professional image that says you are serious about doing an exemplary job.

Tips for More Confident Presentations

First and foremost, your goal is not to *close* a sale during your presentation but to *open* a relationship that lasts for years. This viewpoint is effective and helps take the pressure off of trying to make a quick sale.

- Prospects can tell if you are just *selling*, but they can also tell if you are excited about making their lives easier. At the end of a presentation, would you like to hear, "This special is just for today so let's write your order now so you can take advantage of it?" Or, while you are in front of your prospects, you say, "This new process should shave at least an hour off of your information-gathering time each day. I would be happy to get you started." Now that can give a presenter confidence! Who would not want the extra time for other job duties!

- Demonstrations, audience participation, and true stories give credibility; can be fun and informative; and help your audience relate to why they should also buy from you. There is a very valid reason why stores serve very tasty samples as they know that if customers have the opportunity to try before they buy, they are encouraged to purchase the product.

- Apply a lubricant like Vaseline (just a dab) on your top teeth so your lips will not get stuck in that rather amusing position.

- With mouth closed, swallow hard while slightly extending your chin outward. This can be done in a way that is not noticeable and helps clear your throat for a stronger voice.

- Be warm, engaging, serious when necessary, maintain good eye contact, and exhibit the utmost in sincerity.

Professional Presenters and Engaged Listeners

Figure 6.1 Professional presenters

If you want to provide engaging and memorable presentations, newsletters, and blogs, here are key elements to success:

Is the Title of Your Presentation Interesting?

If you saw your title for the first time, would it catch your attention? Your first goal is to capture their attention and make them want to listen further or read on. Does the title reflect the value and benefits they will ultimately receive? Spend time creating an interesting title. You might need to write your message first before determining what title will be most effective. That is okay and often gives you a better *feel* for how to initially grab their interest. Try a few titles on friends or associates first to learn what is most appealing to the majority.

Belief, Passion, and Commitment—Does Yours Show?

Passion, enthusiasm, and your belief in your message can make a statement like nothing else. When you are passionate, enthusiastic, and committed to share an authentic, meaningful life or career-transforming message, your audience and readers are much more likely to become engaged in your message. Show that you truly believe your product, service, book, or whatever it is will save them time and money, help guide them in a new direction, create a more engaged workforce, and so on. Offer statistics, samples, photos, or videos and testimonies.

Pack a Powerful Punch: Use Stories and Facts to Educate and Influence

Influential presenters and writers use stories, hypothetical situations, or relevant examples to help their audiences relate personally and professionally. Stories are interesting and add a very *human* touch to our day-to-day world. Be sure your stories and examples strengthen your point.

One copy machine representative gave a presentation to the heads of the purchasing department, finance and acquisitions, human resources, accounting, and a few administrative staff. He brought a large piece of brown paper with a picture of the machine and set it on the floor where the new machine would go if purchased. He gave them a visual picture of benefits and conveniences they would receive at that specific location. By the time he helped them visualize the new equipment sitting there and all of the benefits, they all agreed it was well worth the investment. Helping buyers or listeners *see* the benefits will often land the sale.

What to Do Before a Successful Presentation

Rehearse Your Presentation

Try to rehearse your presentation in front of an audience, even if a friend or partner. If it relates to teenagers or the elderly, for instance, get one or two individuals from that age group. If no one is available, record yourself and then sit quietly, watching for adjustments for improvement. Be open to gaining valuable insights regarding what needs to be changed or improved. If you are not able to rehearse in front of someone, verbalize your presentation out loud, preferably in front of a full-length mirror. Monitor your volume, tone, and gestures. Videotaping and reviewing your presentation is tremendously helpful.

Actively Move

Engage in some form of physical exercise to release endorphins, which will make you happier. You will feel less stressed and more confident talking in front of others. Smile. Take deep breaths.

Walk Around the Room or Auditorium Before Your Presentation

As you walk around the room, check to make sure all attendees will have verbal and visual access to you or your charts, PowerPoint, informational materials, and so on.

Familiarize Yourself With the Stage or Presentation Area

See how much room you have to move in. Walk around to get you into *speaking mode* and the right mindset for delivering an engaging talk or discussion. Look at the empty chairs in the conference room or auditorium and *see* them filled in your mind. Keep your chin up and parallel to the floor. Roll your shoulders back and drop them down in a confident stance. Open your arms to your invisible audience as if welcoming them in. This will help build confidence and comfort.

Check Your Equipment

Ensure all technology is in good working order. This includes visuals like PowerPoint and a microphone that transmits sound effectively. Note: Always have a copy of all of your presentation in written form in case technical equipment breaks down at the last minute or the host forgot to take care of an important detail. Yes, this really does happen. Attendees are there to *listen* to you, not watch a slideshow.

Rehearse Your Opening Until It Is Smooth

Although you do not memorize your entire presentation, ensure that your opening has been well rehearsed so you start speaking directly to your listeners and not reading your introduction. It will be easier to overcome any stage fright because you will already know what to say as you set the stage for what they will learn.

Preparation Before Speaking

Try to break away and listen to some soothing music, meditate for a few minutes, or close your eyes and visualize you confidently presenting on stage or at the front of a room. This will help keep calm and focused.

Visualize Your Presentation Being a Success

From world-class athletes and pageant contestants visualizing themselves as winners, each has spent a phenomenal amount of time visualizing their victory. This helps them *get in the zone* and focus. Visualize yourself giving a great presentation and handling any unexpected challenges with ease and confidence.

Prepare for Questions and Issues That may Arise

Take time to determine what questions or even controversial issues could arise so that you have any necessary statistics or stories that will solidify your stance.

In a Nutshell

- Rehearse your presentation
- Move around and get some physical exercise
- Explore the room you will be speaking in
- Become familiar with the stage
- Check and familiarize yourself with all equipment
- Rehearse the opening of your presentation so your eyes are on the attendees
- Listen to some music, meditate, or whatever helps you relax
- Visualize your presentation and audience engagement.

Connecting with the Minds of Your Audience

- Ensure everything you say and all materials presented are relevant information delivered at the right time to the right group and industry. Consider what is best to say—and not to say. Speakers who only think about themselves as being the center of attention may lose that attention. The audience is the center of attention, so everything said must be of benefit to them. This definitely applies when speaking to family and friends as far as ensuring key points are relevant to that particular conversation.
- A winning presentation style. Distracting mannerisms, verbal fidgeting (ums, ahs), and nervous pacing all detract from the speaker's credibility. A major part of your goal is for the audience to relax and absorb what you say and not share nervousness or discomfort.
- Carefully design your talk with all points in order so that the audience does not need to expend energy trying to piece

together bits of information. One example is to take a problem and then go step by step, in proper sequence, to reach the resolution.

- Properly designed graphics. All graphics should accompany the exact comments being made. They must be clear, concise, and ones the audience does not have to guess at what they mean. One example for a financial person is to show a graphic of a frustrated person looking over a stack of bills on the left and then a happy, triumphant person on the right possessing something that reveals victory.

- Consistent attention to audience needs. An audience member who is thirsty, hungry, deprived of caffeine, or in need of a break has a difficult time listening, let alone focusing and retaining your information. Watch them and see if they need to do an interactive exercise or have a short question and answer session to reactivate their brain.

- Demonstrate respect for an audience of any size, even one person. Most people will overlook a less-than-perfect presentation style if the content is valuable or interesting. Listeners have every right to expect a presentation with good content and excellent delivery. You may have a presentation that basically goes to a variety of different audiences, so always modify it according to the socio-economic and age group you are with.

- Ensure you provide top-rated service your audience expects. Consider the importance of breaks, water, and participation. As the old saying goes, "The mind can only absorb what the seat can tolerate."

Emotion, a Key Player to Engaging Your Listeners (of Any Age)

Even for the most analytical person, there are always underlying emotions that will surface. These emotions run the gamut from issues involving money and finances, how others relate to them, what successes and failures they think about, hardships that affected their lives, and a world of other thoughts. Again, watch their faces and body signals to see what works to keep them engaged.

A specific emotion can be triggered instantly without even having to think about the comment made or scenario that was set. We find ourselves responding to a threat even before we are consciously aware of it. Think of jumping back when we see a sudden movement in front of us or being startled by the sound of a loud noise. We also respond instantaneously to positive stimulus without thinking about it, like smiling back (or frowning) when someone smiles (or frowns) at us first. Ever notice how you can be immediately distracted when something you consider beautiful enters your line of sight? Become very aware of your emotions in all situations. You will find it fascinating.

Quick review: Always watch the audience's emotional response and how they are connecting with you. What words, emotions, and stories are grabbing their attention? What expressions and body language are they exhibiting? Does it call for any adjustments in your talk? If so, switch it up a bit to better relate. Offer more statistics, visual aids, or whatever you feel would be of benefit.

Before Speaking—to Eat or Not to Eat

- Avoid high-carbohydrate foods, which can cause you to feel tired or foggy.
- Before important presentations or meetings, skip any foods with excessive roughage, like wheat products. Many carbohydrates can stick in the throat, causing you to stop for a drink of water.
- Avoid extremely hot or cold beverages just before you face an audience. Cold constricts the throat muscles and heat expands them.
- Dairy products before speaking tend to thicken mucus in your throat, causing you to hesitate or stop for a drink of water.
- It may be helpful to slowly sip a warm cup of tea with honey and lemon or a slightly flat cola at room temperature before speaking. Ahhh!
- Resting before an important meeting helps give a tired presenter a second wind.

Strategies for Audience Engagement

Figure 6.2 Strategies for audience engagement

If speaking to audiences that are under stress due to changes within the company, tired of overtime, or distracted by a tough situation, the presenter is wise to take those issues into consideration:

1. *Establish a nonverbal (body signals) connection* before beginning to speak. If you have the opportunity to be at the back of the room to meet attendees before you speak, ask them what they particularly came there to hear. Give a powerful and warm greeting followed by silence while making eye contact from one side of the room to the other. Do you need to grab their attention with a powerful or motivating statement or an appropriate joke or story?

2. *Begin with the most important point first once you have their attention.* This should be a weighty, defining statement that will control the

direction of the rest of your presentation. I once heard a man begin with "By the age of 16, I had been kicked out of every junior high and high school in the city." After that, he followed up with facts and true, relevant stories.

3. Bring your presentation full circle as you repeat your powerful defining statement at the close of your talk. "Thank you all for your active participation, offering effective and relevant suggestions to meet our goals this quarter, and for the overtime you so willingly did. Enjoy breakfast tomorrow in the lunchroom. We appreciate you!"

4. *Make it easy to remember.* Our electronic age fills life with so many issues simultaneously. This can often make it difficult for people to hear, become engaged in what is being said, and then remember key points. The audience needs to hear important facts and details at least three times. You can change how you to say it, but the points themselves must stay consistent. One time you can talk about a specific point through statistics, the next time use that same point in a story, and then finally stress the same point with an emotion, and so on.

5. *Connect an emotion* to anything you want individuals to wrap their minds around. True stories, actual cases (personal, legal, financial, organizational) that pertain to your points are very effective. Sharing experiences that you and especially other listeners have experienced add value as well.

Use Your Body Signals to Help You and Your Audience Connect

Body signals can help calm or excite an audience. They will subconsciously react to what your body says in addition to what your words relay.

Stand grounded with feet apart in a confident and secure position unless seated at the head of the table. Gain more presence by extending your elbows out to the sides. This lends to your impression of being a trustworthy and steady speaker, increasing your credibility. Avoid stances that show nervousness: feet touching or crossed, leaning on the podium, or fidgeting with your hands or clothing. Walking back and forth in a room or on stage shows energy, but pacing quickly from one end to the other shows nervousness or that the speaker is unsure of his or her information. Rapid movements, whether sitting or standing, reveal a presenter who is uncomfortable with either the subject matter or the audience. Display immediate confidence by practicing your opening until it becomes smooth and self-assured.

Move with purpose. Many speakers move without purpose, either through nervousness or an attempt to be electrifying. These are the ones who wander while looking around, *strut their stuff,* or shift back and forth. Use your body to emphasize important points. Moving constantly becomes distracting and literally can cause the audience to become restless.

Aid comprehension by moving to three different spots, each one representing a specific point. Possibly stand in the middle for Point #1, then walk to the right each time you speak of Point #2, and the left each time you refer to Point #3. This actually helps solidify each point, better enables listeners to grasp them logically, and boosts retention. Also, follow this if using a whiteboard.

Engaging Your Audience

Is there any way you can involve your listeners by asking an opening question? Can you have them participate in a short activity to get the blood flowing, especially after a meal when there is a tendency to be drowsy. Interactive versus a straight lecture can be very powerful, keeping the group energetically engaged and feeling like part of the whole.

Visuals and Comparisons

Using visual images and similarities relevant to your message is an effective way to help your audience see and understand more about your topic and why it is important for them to know. That is because we all have a dominant way of learning as well as a secondary one. Always remember that some learn more by hearing (aural), some by seeing (visual), and others by doing (kinesthetic). Some like stories and others want facts. I have had that challenge of a mixed audience more than once. On one occasion, I was asked to give a presentation to a college where the room consisted of everyone from the custodial staff to the president and vice presidents of the college. Challenging? Yes. Doable? Absolutely. It took a variety of facts, figures, stories, demonstrations, and interacting with attendees.

Exhibit, Instruct, Display

For those who abhor reading directions on a box but would rather have someone show them or look at the pictures, visual demonstrations and experiences help with retention. For those who like to read, short key bullet points will help fill the bill. Handouts may sometimes need to be emailed ahead of time, but many speakers prefer to disseminate them, by hardcopy or e-mail, afterward so that the audience is not reading instead of listening.

Provide suggested steps to success with additional people, places, and resources that will further their goals with your new information. These can include creators and designers, distributors, happy customers, motivated employees … the list is endless.

How to Read Your Audience

Those silent, yet very loud, signals from your audience are indicators that tell you if attendees are present in mind or in body only. Whether the audience consists of one person listening to your sales presentation, or a room of 500 people from your industry, following these tips will help you present a more engaging session and help build your reputation as a confident, credible speaker.

- *Unreceptive or dismissing:* Individuals from all socio-economic and age groups can exhibit signs of passive rejection to create distance between the two of you. Their eyes wander to cellphones, bodies slump and turn away from you, they fidget or shut their notebook. At this point, it is necessary to re-engage them by asking a question, walking around if in a room where you may do so, or bringing a bit of appropriate humor into your message.
- *Nonverbal messages can diffuse hostility* by maintaining a composed demeanor. Restraining your own body language

Figure 6.3 How to read your audience

when someone is angry with you can actually have a calming effect on them. Keep your voice low, yet firm, and limit gestures while preserving a relaxed posture to discourage others from a potential rant.

- *Sitting:* An individual sitting on the edge of the chair appears to be in a hurry to leave and may not be paying attention. If their lower back is pressed against the back of their chair while head and shoulders are leaning slightly forward, most likely, they are absorbed in your conversation.
- *Crossing body parts:* Sometimes, this signal just says that they are cold or do not know what to do with their arms. Crossing arms and legs while turning away is a signal they have shut you out. Reconnect with them in your presentation.
- *Facial expression:* A smile shows warmth and interest. A deer-in-the-headlights look signals they might not understand your point. Even if they are too embarrassed to ask a question, be sure to clarify your point to (1) avoid

misunderstandings, (2) the audience leaving without *getting it*, or (3) people departing in disagreement with no further chance to find out why.

- *Tilting the head:* When listeners tilt their heads to the side, it is usually a good sign they are intently listening. When it is your turn to speak, however, be sure your head is straight with chin parallel to the floor to exude the most confidence.

- *Nodding in agreement:* Studies have shown that when a man nods his head to a woman, he is most likely signaling that what a woman said is acknowledged, and that is the end of the conversation, or at least that point. Quite often when a woman nods her head to a man, she is actually indicating to him to "Go on, I'm listening," which means she wants more information. Always clarify the point is understood and agreed upon (even if you agree to disagree) before going to the next part.

Bottom line: Always check to ensure your body is saying the same thing as your mouth. Your goal is to have the most clear, concise, and confident presentation possible.

Leading the Way: Your Ticket for Becoming an Indispensable Success

Consider these important aspects of the indispensable person everyone wants to be around: Allowing for emotion (within appropriate boundaries), sentiment, strength, differences in temperament, compassion, empathy, kindness, and concern. These do not show weakness; they show true strength personally and professionally!

Exceptional Leadership Can Be Recognized in Any Position

Good leaders have the ability to both lead and follow. They are visionaries who can influence individuals to *do things*. They have a high sense of integrity and use wisdom in their decision making. Successful influencers are not always popular but will act for the greater good. They hold their ground when necessary. Being favorably sought after also commands being humble enough to make corrections if someone else offers a better solution.

Critical characteristics include the ability to stay focused on the final outcome while giving support to those involved. It incorporates the heart as well as the head in decision making and problem solving. Leaders see themselves as *resources*, not just *bosses*.

Male or female power differences: At times, women believe they must develop the characteristics that work for men if they want to operate in a leadership position. Although women can learn valuable lessons from the male perspective, they are not meant to behave like men. Women have a distinctive way of processing information, motivating, and multitasking all at the same time. They can provide a congenial atmosphere where employees feel appreciated and listened to. This is an important key to loyalty. They do not need to forsake their femininity for ambition. They can be successful in their own right, walking in the flow of the talents they were born with.

The male approach is more often defined as someone who is willing to take charge, is competitive, and is able to understand and play company politics. Female attributes include intuition, a care-and-share attitude, open communications, establishing and maintaining relationships with others. These are important leadership strengths that benefit everyone. Female intuition is an asset that enhances one's ability to sense approaching problems and opportunities. This does not mean forsaking the need to take charge or compete for business, as those traits are very important.

Following are other characteristics that affect our indispensable standing: Leading by example, directing, controlling a situation we are in charge of (not being a controller), managing, steering, guiding, preceding, going in front of. Additional traits include being a frontrunner, trailblazer, groundbreaker, advisor, or mentor.

1. What kind of people do you prefer to follow?
2. What kind of leadership behaviors do you find defeating, defensive, or demoralizing?
3. Which of the following behaviors resonate with you and motivate you to excel, take risks, and grow stronger?

Rational: Sensible, logical, realistic, balanced. These are excellent traits, but must be mixed with heart and emotion for the most effective influence.

Judgmental: Critical, negative, disapproving, takes offense easily, resentment. We have all worked with or for someone in management and co-worker roles who exhibited these behaviors. This causes very low morale and disengagement, affecting lives, productivity, and certainly the bottom line.

Mind: Aware, observe, notice, think, intellect, opinion, attitude, belief, conviction. Our beliefs, opinions, and convictions play a major part in the decisions we make, whether beneficial or detrimental, and affect every part of our lives. Always consider those who will be involved.

We hold important positions by positive reinforcement, reassurance, and inspiration, not by instilling fear or trying to control. Other key attributes include bravery when necessary, fortitude, and pluck (determination, resolve). It is our center, our core, the basis of all that is *us*. No wonder our hearts are so affected by the everyday issues of life, as we strive to lead ourselves, our families and those we work with down a productive, successful path. This incorporates not allowing preconceived ideas, fears, and personal opinions to cloud our judgment.

A very important question to ask yourself is "Am I operating in fear, frustration, questioning my abilities to rise above my competition? Am I wondering what they really think of me?" or "Am I effectively using my intellect, gifts, and talents while still allowing my heart and mind to influence my decisions and behaviors?"

Rejection is a part of life, personally and professionally. How does one successfully manage rejection? Rejection is a word we all know well. It can happen in an instant or simmer in someone's mind for months before it causes them to push away, get angry, break off a relationship (in business, social, or personal life), or do something not in the best interest of all involved. Successfully overcoming rejection requires a healthy self-esteem to view the situation and the person's response from the most beneficial standpoint. Avoid letting it influence how you see your value as a person or a leader. Take time to assess the situation from your angle, their angle, and what a third party may see as the reasons for the rejection or refusal.

Not all leaders or sought-after individuals are in actual designated *leadership positions*. We all have the opportunity to be an effective leader every day, in whatever capacity the day calls for, whether at home or with those who have a broad influence in our world. This powerful way to lead requires the ability to listen. If that is difficult due to preconceived ideas operating in our conscious mind (our own opinions or too many distractions), then make it your goal to learn how to really pay attention and listen. This necessitates being willing to clear personal obstacles like your own story and beliefs as well as any difficulties within the company where management or performance issues might throw obstacles in your way. Practice staying strong and focused.

In what ways have you experienced these characteristics in a positive or negative light? By others? By yourself? Think about each of the following and how you want to use these traits, as well as their possible outcomes, from this day forward. These apply to children and individuals of all ages and backgrounds as well.

- *Directing*: Producing, regulating, controlling, showing the way, putting on the right track, pointing, targeting, training
- *Controlling*: Running, commanding, ruling, manipulating, in charge of (running a company most definitely does not include manipulating, for instance)
- *Managing*: Administrating, overseeing, accomplishing, bossing, dominating
- *Steering*: Pushing, driving, guiding
- *Guiding*: Showing, shepherding, steering
- *Preceding*: Going in front of, scoping out new territory or opportunities
- *Differentiation*: What differentiates a heart-centered leader or employee from one who operate strictly from a rational mindset? Which of their characteristics attracted you? Repelled you?

In a study with several thousand people, individuals were asked to describe their best bosses. Over and over, the respondents said things like, "I rarely talked to her" or "He left you alone," or "She gave you total freedom to get the job done how you saw fit." Step aside and let competent workers do what they do best. Keep your door open, instruct, and guide, but do not micromanage. The first step in empowering people is to refrain from doing anything that reduces authority, energy, and enthusiasm!

Invaluable owners, operators and employees, friends, and family have a heart–mind connection. They are not expecting to be served, but to work alongside. They provide others the opportunity to learn, grow, and make decisions. They tell the truth, even if it is difficult and may upset someone. Truth always wins in the long run. It not only influences others to trust us and want to work with us, but we gain much more respect for not twisting the truth for our own benefit.

These individuals are not quick to rush into judgment or make assumptions, but instead make every effort to understand the entire situation and motives as well as what may be going on in that person's life. This includes asking appropriate and relevant questions to get the full picture. What happened? How did the behavior or words make all involved feel? How did the misunderstanding take place? Was it a sharp look or comment? Were we automatically dismissed without being heard?

When we practice the characteristics of an indispensable person by positive example, we show the world what we are truly made of: grit, determination, fair mindedness, sensitivity, and a can-do attitude.

Figure 6.4 Value

Use the following list of characteristics as a guide and worksheet. Take each attribute and score yourself on where you are now. Thoughtfully write the steps you believe will get you to the place where you truly want to be. This will take time but is more than worth it.

Affirmations or appreciation: Sincere praise and appreciation shows confidence in your abilities and position. Single out those who have gone the extra mile and make them feel so good about what they did that they cannot wait to do it again. Recognize them at the next department meeting or send a letter to the general manager or company president letting them know of their contributions. Seeing this recognition can encourage the entire staff to seek new opportunities to go the extra mile. A motivated staff is a powerful staff! Take care to *notice* positive behavior and make it a regular part of your entire business. The more you thank other people for doing things for you, the more they will want to do. That is admirable leadership!

Appearance, you and your personal brand: Clothing should help you move up socially and in business, not hold you back! Appearance can work for you by projecting a polished, confident image, or work against you by having scuffed, run-down shoes, wrinkled clothing, or unkempt fingernails. Signs that show a lack of concern in appearance can indicate low self-esteem, carelessness, or that there is no motivation to go any further in life. You always want to be recognized as the polished, intelligent, and articulate professional, rather than remembered for an appearance inconsistent with your position. Dress for comfort, but also to exhibit respect, power, and confidence. Remember, anyone in any position can be a leader!

Attitude: Negative or fearful thoughts keep us stuck. Self-absorbed individuals tend to dominate conversations and see others only as a comment to get what they want. This is not only unattractive, it is detrimental to one's own personal development. Self-absorbed people tend to have poor relationships, whereas a leader who instills a can-do attitude into a team can move mountains!

Collaborative: Collaboration provides powerful synergy. Effective collaboration includes leading by example, having good reasoning skills, and never conforming on an issue just to please others in order to succeed. They like to create a sense of *community*, help preserve memories, and be part of something bigger than themselves.

Commitment To excellence: Without commitment, there can be no success. Without commitment, tough times can pull you away to an easier path. Great leaders lead by example and build trust in those who work with them. Trust allows others to disagree when necessary and not just echo what everyone thinks the individual at the top wants to hear. Although you must listen to, and respect, other's opinions, giving in or compromising your values. Frontrunners *inspire* those around them. The key is commitment.

Competence: You *know* you have the ability to get the job done. You are the confident leader who produces results. This may take some strong self-talk at times. Do it.

Confidence: One major example of confidence is being secure enough to apologize when wrong. People often need a self-confidence boost and that boost increases self-esteem. People tend to treat us the way we treat ourselves, so speak and act with self-assurance. Great leaders are humble *and* confident. *The most important thing a person can wear is confidence!*

Consistency: When many difficult occurrences are raging around us, it can be difficult to maintain consistent behavior. There is nothing worse than wondering what kind of mood a boss or co-worker will be in when you arrive at work. Keep in mind that people in any position do not like being treated like *light switches,* where the boss turns them on when he or she wants something, then ignores them until something is needed again. This sends a clear message that they are being taken for granted, and that the leader or manager just does not care. Once people receive this message, they become *turned off* to continue going the extra mile.

Conflict—do not avoid it, embrace it: Frontrunners resolve conflict by analyzing, listening, and working through the situation. Conflict can generate new ideas that leaders can then bring to the table. I read where a woman who received a promotion knew that one man would not support her, so her first thought was to avoid dealing with him. When she discovered that he was starting a new project for the company, she wrote to him pledging her department would do anything they could to support the project. She turned the relationship around. Be creative and powerful in your conflict resolution!

Conviction: Leaders must maintain a strong backbone. Stand for what is right, even if it is not looked upon favorably. Be confident in your convictions and major goals, willing to take the risks necessary to support them and to establish respect.

Courage: Successful leaders must develop courage to ensure their team has the resources they need and to resist conforming to a leadership style that is not their own. Be willing to lead collaboratively if that is *your* style, even if it is not the one modeled at the top.

Courtesy and respect—treat people politely: Treating people poorly suggests a tremendous lack of integrity. We cannot lead well if we do not know what is going on in the trenches, where business connections are created and deals are sealed. People do things because they either want to or because they have to. Kindness, courtesy, and respect make them *want* to do things for us. They are motivated to go out of their way to help solve problems and accomplish our goals. Being nice to other people makes them feel important and respected. It is one of the most critical aspects of a quality owner, manager, or employee.

Criticism—constructive or destructive: There is a proverb that says, "Listen to advice and accept instruction and in the end, you will be wise." In meetings, a cooperative, open-minded, and constructive approach to problem solving accomplishes so much more than angry, defensive behavior.

Empowering others—give them freedom to excel: Empower comments means *putting power into*, and it can also mean *bringing energy and enthusiasm out of.* There is something liberating and energizing when we have been entrusted with a major responsibility and given the freedom to fulfill it. When the right person has been matched with the right job, the conditions for exceptional performance have been created. *Expect* success! Positive expectations show your belief in their ability to succeed. The strong leader (regardless of what position they hold) will influence the mental and emotional atmosphere for the whole organization. Project a positive attitude, no matter how distressing the situation appears. Always strive for complete control of yourself and your emotions.

High stress levels have been traced to a national trend toward controlling behavior. Controlling people concern themselves not only with their own thoughts and actions, but insist others think and act in certain ways as well. This is a losing battle, as there is usually more than one approach to doing things.

Inspire: Inspire others to peak performance. A transformational worker is one who excites and inspires people to perform far beyond their own expectations of themselves. They practice behaviors that cause others to feel stronger, happier, more confident, and committed.

Integrity and truth-telling: Our integrity is revealed in our daily actions and reactions on the job. It originates from the heart, not from a desire to gain an advantage over others. An example would be to never pass the buck to cover up our own mistakes. We must be accountable, admitting our mistakes, and seeking to rectify them. Even when we are discouraged and tempted to give up or compromise our integrity, we stick to our principles. When tempted, remember this quote by an unknown individual: "A person's wardrobe tells you what he or she *does*, but their walks in life tells you what they *are*." When people are asked what trait they most want in a leader, integrity and honesty generally top the list. Studies have shown that indispensable individuals bring to boardrooms an increased focus on ethics and positive authority. When the people around you know that you are a person of integrity, they know you can add value to their lives and not worry about your motives. They trust you. In everything you do involving other people, you are shaping and influencing their perceptions of you and the position you hold in their minds.

Lead by example: Indispensables are known for jumping in and doing what needs to be done. This reflects great inner strength with an added plus of having an extensive world view.

Leadership strategies and outcomes: The impact of an indispensable has no bounds! An ancient quote from Phillip II of Macedon still holds true today: "An army of deer led by a lion is more to be feared than an army of lions led by a deer." Why? A lion is involved, firm and confident, always scouting new opportunities for provisions. They take position for battle *and* they take care of their own. Deer are peaceful, passive … and run away when frightened. Indispensables hold their chins up and move forward.

Nurture and inspire: You can be a vital member without degrading others as you move forward, whether in a career or as a coach. Always be mindful of other's feelings and never jump to conclusions about their behavior. No one knows what challenges they may be dealing with. Show that you care by finding out what is happening with them and be supportive.

Passion: Passion increases willpower and determination. It gives you the will to move on when you want to quit. It changes you. In the end, your passion will have more influence than your personality. It makes the impossible possible. A leader with great passion and few skills always outperforms a leader with great skills but no passion. Your best chance at success is through doing work you love. If you are not happy in your chosen field, consider switching to one for which you have a genuine interest or passion.

Perception is reality: The perception people have of your performance capabilities exerts a great influence on how they think and feel about you as a leader or team member in any capacity. Sometimes, a reputation for being excellent at what you do can be so powerful that it alone can make you an extremely persuasive individual with those around you.

They accept your advice, are open to your influence, and agree with your requests. People act on the basis of their perceptions of you. If you appear, by your mannerisms, wardrobe, grooming, and communication skills, to be a high-ranking leader or a person of influence, they are much more likely to help you than if you were perceived to be a lower-level employee.

Power—be comfortable with yours! Power struggles are evident everywhere, whether in running a household or managing a business. These struggles often do not show up in a blatant manner, but in daily activities like meetings, decision making, and conversations. It is a strongly motivated attempt to acquire control, authority, or influence over a person, situation, or thing. This is not a very becoming trait and does not show strength of character. Consider the good of the whole picture. Ask for what you aspire to, whether it is asking for a raise, more resources for a project, or for a second chance. It is amazing what you can accomplish simply by asking for what you want and including a benefit, problem resolution, or whatever is applicable. The key is to believe in your request and that others want to help you. They will *feel* your true beliefs by the energy you project.

Satisfy the deepest needs: The deepest need each person has is for a sense of feeling important, valuable, and worthwhile. Everything that you do in your interactions with others affects your self-esteem, and theirs, in some way. Give to others first what you want in return.

Share, request, information: Essential partners in our global community should also be a good followers and careful listeners. It is in expressing oneself honestly that we earn trust. We tactfully clear the air so that discord and resentment do not get a foothold. A good way to destroy a project or relationship is for the members to not communicate. Be the catalyst to open the channels of communication.

Visionary: Create a shared vision for home as well as work. Keep your organization focused on what is most important and communicate it in a meaningful, memorable way. Share the vision in terms that the team can visualize. See everything you do in terms of the larger picture, for the greater good.

Characteristics of Sought-After Relationships: No Matter What Position You Hold!

Loyalty, a person's best friend. What does it mean for family, friends, associates, and clients to be loyal to you? Basically, the same traits others require of you as well.

1. They accept you with your strengths—and weaknesses.
2. They speak well of you to others. Loyal people may disagree with you *privately* and hold you accountable for what you are capable of achieving, yet they never criticize you to others.
3. They are able to share the ups and downs as you journey together, making the trip less lonely and much more fulfilling.
4. They share your dream by taking ownership in their work and behavior and sharing your journey. A special few will want to come alongside and help you reach the finish line.

Now what?

Write a job description for a fantastic boss and use it as a guide for yourself. Be the one who gives honest feedback, is patient of other's mistakes, does not overload employees, and realizes they have lives outside of work. Be the kind of boss you would want to work for.

Making things happen in and through others mainly depends on your ability to relate to them. Without trustworthiness and respect, there is no unity, and people go their own way. If your dream is big and requires the

Figure 6.5 Groucho Marx

teamwork of a lot of people, those you select to work with will need to be people who are upright, loyal, supportive, and can develop the ability to influence others. That is what being indispensable is all about. When you think about it, all leaders have two things in common: (1) They are going somewhere and (2) they are able to persuade others to go along with them. Thomas Jefferson once said, "No duty the executive has to perform is so trying as to put the right man in the right place." Prove you are the right person in the right place.

As the old saying goes, "Today is the first day of the rest of your life!" Plant seeds of exemplary leadership and watch them grow!

CHAPTER 7

Design a Powerful Portfolio: Make Them Want to Do Business With You

Consider yourself as a professional portfolio because you actually are one! Your verbal, nonverbal, and written collection of characteristics and personality traits create a limitless span of perceptions and observations that determine your future direction, relationships, and degree of success.

> ***Become THE ONE. Be all that you want to see in others—courteous, continuously learning, exhibiting a professional appearance. It is in being a dynamic listener who has such excellent conversational skills that your lines of communication are beyond compare!

Create a promotional portfolio that demonstrates your accomplishments, education, experience, and awards into one convenient and efficient package. Such a portfolio is a highly effective marketing tool that gives prospects a complete picture of who you are—your experience, education, achievements, skill sets, and what you have the potential to do for them. Use it to display a point, illustrate the depth of your skills and experience, or as a tool for a second interview. Include anecdotes about *how* you got something done, against whatever odds may have been encountered and what the outcome was.

When creating your portfolio, determine what is something you do better than anyone else you know. What are some examples that verify this? Include news articles featuring something you achieved, white papers, photos, reference letters—whatever gets the job done in a positive manner. Who can you ask to give you references? You can show a history of many years to verify how you have built upon your skills throughout

Figure 7.1 Confident communication

the years. Creating this portfolio can help guide you with what steps to take next and will add another accomplishment to your list.

First, do a self-assessment. List what is interesting about you that you can share with others. *Yes*, you *do* have many interesting (business appropriate) things to share! Put pen to paper and begin listing them. Include your passion for writing, fundraising, organizational skills, creativity, dynamic focus on a particular sport, love of speaking in front of others, and so on. *It is not all about "what" you do but "who" you are as a person!*

What specifically are you are doing, or have done, that will make you interesting? Engaging? Or that validates your experience, knowledge, and why you stand above your competition?

Work on the script until it flows, sounds confident, and depicts the true nature of your business and capabilities. As you meet new clients and build new business relationships, be intent on presenting yourself in a positive manner, upbeat, and confident about your work and life. If you are in the early stages of building a portfolio, just finishing school or switching careers, pull in all of those skills and positions you held that still apply.

- What is the primary value you provide? Are there any additional benefits you could add to your basic services?
- Is it possible to offer more *surprise* value? Helping clients in *unexpected* ways, identifying issues, and solving problems they did not even ask to be addressed can very favorably enhance

your business relationships. Nothing can impress a potential or current client more than someone who has gone beyond the call of duty and exceeded expectations!

- What about investing more *personal* value to clients by coaching or counseling them in ways that will help them further develop their business? This act alone could reap tremendous benefits!

Increasing Resources That Build Stronger Relationships

Take adequate time to dig into this one. What will further set you apart professionally and personally from competitors in the marketplace? Could it be a new idea that saves time and money, or increases productivity? For instance, were you responsible for a memorable, profitable event, or helped launch a new product? Did your awesome gift of showing potential customers all of the benefits *they* would enjoy on their new computer put you at the top of the customer service representatives?

What will you do next year to be even more memorable and more distinctive? Is it possible to provide something that is ultimately more appealing to clients? This is part of a successful business plan. Ask those who already do business with you what would be most beneficial to them in the coming six months, then determine if you can do it.

Recommendations and Referrals

Ask others to give you an endorsement of your product or service. Seek testimonials, referrals, and references to verify your talent, product quality, or exceptional service. Create a portfolio of written and videotaped recommendations to share with prospects; build your reputation; and to gain new and happy clients, employees, participants, or readers! Ensure the pages have consistent headlines, type styles, and colors.

What specifically are you are doing, or have done, that will make you interesting? Engaging? That validates your experience, knowledge, and why you stand above your competition?

Work on the script until it flows, sounds confident, and depicts the true nature of your business and capabilities. As you meet new clients and build new business relationships, be intent on presenting yourself in a positive manner, upbeat, and confident about your work and life.

Write out and practice introducing yourself to a variety of individuals from various industries. What are the key points you will mention?

Following is a checklist to use for your visual portfolio until these habits become second nature. Record your thoughts on each point. What can you do to make your professional image even better?

- Stand in a front of a full-length mirror before leaving home and take a close look at your appearance. It is the only way to be sure that the look you have achieved is the one you want to project to the world. Are there any areas that need improvement?
- Remember that clothes reflect your personality and commitment to doing a good job. Are they simple, tailored, and attractive without being distracting? What is the message you are projecting? Does it say you are serious, yet friendly and professional, or does it say you are seriously thinking about meeting friends after work?
- Your hairstyle and clothing choices really do send out messages. Start looking around. What do you see?
- Are accessories more appropriate for a date or party than for the workplace? Switch out pieces for other events after work if need be.
- Carefully listen to your voice whether speaking in person or on the phone. Record it for a day or two and then listen to yourself. Is it strong and clear or is there a nasal sound? Does it have a deep, rich quality or sound high-pitched, thin, or weak? Would you like to listen to this voice? If the answer is *no*, practice controlling your pitch, rate, tone, and overall voice quality until the answer is *yes*.
- Are you at your best, ready to do business with anyone, no matter who they are or what position they hold? If not, what steps can be taken to get there? Write them down.

Review

Again, ask yourself, "If I were viewing myself from another person's perspective, would I want to do business with me?" Why or why not? Would my appearance, manner, and speech exhibit the kind of characteristics that would prompt you to do business with myself? Why or why not? Have your discovered areas you would still like to change? What behaviors are you now confident in? Smile!

> Bottom line, technical skills are not the only requirement for new or continued business opportunities. Good soft skills are critical for taking us where we want to go in life and in business.
>
> You are the architect of your life and career. Every day, think and see yourself as an indispensable powerhouse, more than capable of shining in this global economy!

Action Plans to Initiate

Now that you have read the book, what changes have you made along the way? What did you learn? How and what will you shift? What are 10 things you can change to walk in your new destiny?

List life circumstances and the feelings you discovered that needed to be altered in order to create your dream and unleash your destiny. Include

1. Why the change was necessary
2. When it happened
3. How did you react
4. Your outcome!

See your beautiful new life's picture developing right before your eyes!

1. _____

2. _____

3. _____

4. _____

5. _____

6. _____

7. _____

8. _____

9. _____

10. _____

Your new mantra for the rest of your life: I am Indispensable—I am Unshakeable—I am Unstoppable!!

When you fall, fall forward! Why? Because when you raise your head, you are facing your future. Advance forward into new territory. Invite others to come along beside you! Lead with your strong, pliable heart!

# # #

About the Author

Rita Rocker is an international published author, life-transforming inspirational and educational speaker, communications and image specialist, and career consultant with SoaringHigher.rocks. She is the creator and host of Transformation Now! KPAO on YouTube. Rita is a former Mrs. Nebraska and Mrs. America contestant. She is a Board member of Transformation Omaha and a member of Professional Woman Network International (PWN) and American Writers and Art Institute (AWAI).

Rita inspires individuals to rise and go forward by providing powerful techniques for victorious personal and professional life makeovers. Clients include women and men from all socio-economic and age groups. She works with individuals, professional organizations, corporations, youth programs, and at conferences and retreats. Rita has appeared on national television and radio talk shows on self-esteem and communication. Her professional background also includes corporate training, human resources, and non-technical project management.

Expertise

- Inspirational and motivating self-esteem programs
- Dynamic communication skills for your personal and professional life
- High-quality professional image, business etiquette and social skills for all socio-economic and age groups
- Career development and exceptional leadership coaching
- Successful branding and networking techniques to stay on the cutting edge
- Customer service and relationship building for an incomparable reputation

Keynote and Breakout Topics Include

- The Whole Enchilada: Creating New Recipes for Your Life
- Marketing Yourself for Success
- Attitudes That Overcome: Triumphing Through Transition
- Be the Brand Everyone is After
- You, Getting Older? You're Just Getting Started!

Rita is the author of: *Creating Your Own Destiny: Power Steps for Mind-Body Renewal; Hope at the End of Your Rope: Steps to Rebuild Your Life* and *Guide to Marketing Yourself for Success.* She is a contributing international author to: *The Professional Woman: Business, Leadership & Communication; The Professional Woman: Self-esteem, Confidence & Empowerment; Leading From the Heart; Sink, Swim or Float: How to Survive the Trials of Life; The Unstoppable Woman's Guide to Emotional Well Being; Woman Power: Strategies for Female Leadership; The Power of Transformation: Reinventing Your Life; Baby Boomers: Secrets for Life After 50; Tapping Your Inner Vision: Transforming Your Life, Shifting Your Mind; The Self-Esteem Guide for Women: How to Build Confidence; Your Personal GPS: How to Navigate Life's Challenges and Roadblocks; The Woman's Book of Empowerment and Confidence (2016) Daily Affirmations*

SoaringHigher.rocks
www.soaringhigher.rocks
PO Box 541181, Omaha, NE 68154
rita@soaringhigher.rocks
www.soaringhigher.rocks
Transformation Now! KPAO (YouTube)
http://pwnbooks.com/rocker.htm
http://linkedin.com/pub/rita-rocker/1/613/381/

Index